Under the Red Star

Marzelius Hausmann

Known as

Mark Houseman

Under the Red Star

Reverend Marzelius Hausmann

(Known as Mark Houseman)

Copyright © 2018 Mark Houseman
Third Edition. All rights reserved.

First Edition. Published by Author, 1941
Second Edition. Published by Author, 1955

Original copyright©1958, Published by the Author, 418 Behring St. Berne, Ind. Printed by Christian M. Muselman, Economy Printing Concern, Berne, Indiana

No part of this book may be reproduced, stored or transmitted by any means, without written permission of the publisher, except for brief quotations in review.

All scripture quotations used are from the King James Version of The Holy Bible.

ISBN: 13:978-1-948118-13-2
Library of congress Control Number TX 1-640-444 (1958)
Remittance number & date: 480816 (March 5, 1985)
Library of Congress Control Number: 2018932410

* Rabboni Book Publishing Company is owned by the daughter of the author – Josephine (Houseman) Blocher

Rabboni Book Publishing Company

Foreword

To the First Edition

(Printed October 13, 1941)

This little volume presents a striking record of God's dealings with a young man whose life had been dedicated to the Lord by his godly mother in "Bolshevik Russia."

The preserving hand and the providential care of God throughout the bloody Russian Revolution, as well as the lonely months in Siberian exile and the years of starvation and famine, must be regarded as nothing short of a modern miracle.

It was my delightful privilege to read the following pages while they were yet in manuscript form, also to have heard this lecture verbally on several occasions.

May it please God to use this message to the salvation of souls and for the comfort and blessing of His saints.

REV. L. W. FORSMARK
Enchant, Alberta, Canada
October 13, 1941

Foreword

TO THE PRESENT EDITION

(August 1955)

We are delighted to present to the reading public a new edition of the book, *Under the Red Star*. In this volume, the author, Rev. Mark Hausmann, gives the experiences of himself and his family very vividly. The great and many sufferings at the hands of the Bolsheviks and Communists are almost unbelievable and yet they are well documented. In it all is seen the wonderful hand of God who has helped here and there some of His people to escape the cruel hand of the oppressor. Now Rev. Hausmann is in this country and is giving faithful testimony to the saving grace of the Lord Jesus Christ. He can truly say that God never fails and "that all things work together for good to them that love God, to them who are called according to His purpose." Romans 8:28.

Further, Rev. Hausmann indeed can join in with Paul: "Having therefore obtained help of God, I continue..." Acts 26:22.

May the Lord richly bless the efforts of Evangelist Mark Hausmann in this country and may many be turned from darkness to light, to serve the true and the living God in righteousness and true holiness.

>Christian H. Muselman,
>Publisher and Manager
>1955 Light and Hope Publications
>1958 Economy Printing Concern, Inc
>Berne, Indiana

Table of Contents

Chapters   **Page**

Foreword..3
Foreword..4

PART I

I.	The Introduction	7
II.	The Road of Tears	11
III.	Our Life in Exile	19
IV.	Father's Death	23
V.	The Revolution	29
VI.	The Greatest Loss of My Life	35
VII.	Life Without Parents	41
VIII.	Facing Famine in its Grim Reality	45
IX.	Finding A Haven of Refuge	55
X.	On the Road Back to the Ukraine	61
XI.	My Life Amongst Relatives	67
XII.	I Became Self Supporting	73
XIII.	Back Where the Cradle Stood	77
XIV.	Back to Work	81
XV.	On My Holidays	87

PART II

I.	Looking For the New World	107
II.	At Sea	113
III.	In Canada	117
IV.	In the Sanitarium	123
V.	In the School of God	133
VI.	In the Prairie Bible Institute	141
VII.	Back to P. B. I.	147
VIII.	The Year of My Ordination	153
IX.	No More I, But "We"	163
X.	The Pastor's Family	169
XI.	In the United States of America	173
XII.	The Last Chapter	177

Epilogue Written by the author's daughter – Josephine (Houseman) Blocher..................183

Mark Houseman's
Testimony:

"For to me to live is Christ, and to die is gain."
Philippians 1:21.

CHAPTER I

The Introduction

"When it pleased God, who separated me from my mother's womb, and called me by His grace, to reveal his Son in me, that I might preach him among the heathen; immediately I conferred not with flesh and blood..." (Galatians 1:15-16).

This was the testimony of a man who was called to preach the gospel of our Lord Jesus Christ, even the dear apostle Paul. By God's grace, this shall be my testimony throughout the rest of my life, God helping me.

As we turn the dials of our radios these days, our hearts tremble with fear. The question arises – what will Russia do? Or what will the nations do with Russia?

Russia! Oh dark Russia! The land that was soaked with blood over and over again. Looking back upon my life, I can recall similar commotions of war and trembling of heart. The question then was passed from person to person. "What will Russia do? What will become of Russia?" But the big Siberian bear is still devouring much flesh.

Turning my eyes from these clouds of darkness, I can still see rays of light which I enjoyed in my early childhood days. These, my bright days, as well as my days of sorrow, I want to share with you in this book.

I was born in Russia in the state of Minsk, known as White Russia. There upon a little hill covered with fir trees stood a fine, new log house surrounded by a few other buildings and farm implements. Around the door of the house was numerous flowers planted and cared for with all the reverence and care that only a good housewife is able to give.

A bench was placed near the house inviting tried wanderers to sit down and enjoy a quiet rest after a very hot summer day.

Our farm was not so large as we see them on this continent of North America. We had some twenty-four acres of land which in that country was considered a fairly good farm. The products raised there are mainly rye, oats and barley.

Now permit me to introduce you to my family relations. We were what you may call a large family, numbering thirteen souls, composed of father, mother, three girls, which were father's daughters by a former marriage, then my own four sisters Adina, Olga, Herta and Mathilda, my only brother still alive, Fredrick, and myself. I happened to be the sixth born to Mother. After me there were four more boys, but these all died in their infancy, as you will read later in the story.

We lived in the above mentioned home until 1914. Those were indeed the most happy years of my life, loved by all, and perhaps a little spoiled, seeing that I was the youngest in the family. This was because my younger brother, born right next to me, unfortunately scalded himself and died when three years old.

As to our living accommodations, we were not what you may call wealthy people, and not of the poorest either, but in between. My father was a carpenter and my mother was a seamstress, by trade next to farmers as we were known in that district. Unfortunately, my father was a victim of strong drink. This terrible habit of my poor father not only consumed the money, but also marred the happiness of our home and forced many tears from the eyes of my saintly praying mother.

There were other sorrows my dear mother faced with a large family: father away a good deal of the time, and such epidemics as the smallpox, measles, and the scarlet fever, to which the entire family was subject. To my own experience as to the epidemic (scarlet fever) I lost my sight completely for a season. After we had sought all the help the physicians could render, which was of no improvement, then the Great Physician, even the Lord Jesus Christ, was beseeched from whence cometh our help. It was on this wise: One day my grandfather (Mother's father) visited us. While looking at my eyes he said, "I believe the eyes of the boy can be opened." Turning to me he said, "Marzelius (for this is my original name) in a few days you shall see again." This was indeed good news to me, a boy of about five years old. The next morning, just when the sun came up, he took me out and set me on a chair, while he knelt on the ground. Putting his elbows on my knees he prayed, then he blew into my eyes three times in the Name of God the Father, God the Son, and God the Holy Spirit. This was repeated three early mornings in succession in faith believing that the Lord is able. Now, my dear friend, this is my testimony. As a result of this faith and prayer, I have my eyes opened and just as perfectly as ever could be expected. All glory to His precious Name! As in the days of old, according to St. Mark 10:45-52, when blind Bartimeus cried unto the Lord to receive his sight, so did my dear old grandfather appeal to the same all-powerful and living Physician who heard and answered his cry.

CHAPTER II

The Road of Tears

You will recall that the year of 1914 the so-called "First Great War" broke out. Shortly after the outbreak of this World War the Russian Government, under the reign of Czar Nicholas II, issued a decree that all foreigners, though born in Russia, must be exiled to Siberia, in order to clear the war zone of any danger which may arise through these foreigners. This decree came in force during the harvest season of 1914. The harvest that year looked very prosperous, which, of course, made matters even much worse for the departing ones. No favor was granted to the farmer in order that he could gather in his crop and dispose of it; immediate evacuation was demanded. The women and children had to leave at once, while the men-folks remained behind for but a day or so; if perchance they could dispose of some of their goods. Of course the opportunity to sell at that time, when everybody wanted to sell and no one wanted to buy, was poor. When the people which were to remain in the country heard that the foreigners had to leave their homes so suddenly they came with the intentions to take and not to buy things. Some, of course, having sympathy and being honest men, did pay for what they took, but others thought it great joy to plunder and steal to their heart's content without restraint from the government authorities.

We were allowed only our bare necessities such as bedding, food, utensils, and a few household goods usable on the trip. Just before we had to leave, my mother and I went to the garden to have the last look at all the lovely things therein which had cost so much labor and love to dear mother. When she realized the seriousness of it all, she just broke down weeping in heart-breaking cries.

I indeed did try very hard to comfort her as a six year old child, but there was no comfort sufficient enough for that poor broken heart.

Only such a person as my dear mother who knew the Lord Jesus Christ as her personal Savior could find comfort in such as we have in the blessed word of God. I am sure that with David of old she could say, "Yea, though I walk through the valley of the shadow of death, I will fear no evil, for thou art with me; thy rod and thy staff they comfort me." (Psalm 23:4).

The method of our conveyance was rather peculiar. They would load our stuff on the wagons of the Russian farmers living in our village. They then would take us to the next village by the order of the police where we would again reload to the responsibility of that village and thus continue day after day, loading and unloading and loading again.

We had to go without father as far as grandfather's place, about 50 miles east from our place, where daddy caught up with us. There we had grandfather's family join us as they, too, were in the same fate.

Unfortunately, in time of war, we have the experi-ence that people with whom you have lived for many years as friend with friend will turn hostile toward you and regard you as their enemy, not because they hate you, but just because nation against nation is in an uproar. This was the case we experienced. For instance, we were not allowed to stay overnight in their village, not saying anything about their home accommodations, but we would be unloaded somewhere near a village on the field or woods (bush). There we would again the next day be picked up by our new conveyers. We would consider ourselves fortunate to camp near a forest where we could kindle a fire. Oh, how a person appreciates the warmth of fire when you are outdoors day and night for months at a time! This is particularly true when it is late in the fall, as it was in our case at that time.

The forethought and consideration of a Godly mother is wonderful. Just before our departure from our home, mother made large feather ticks which indeed proved a blessing. Every night when we were going to rest, one of these ticks was spread on the ground; then we six youngsters would fit ourselves on it in sardine fashion, one with the head this way and the other that way, in order to make room for all. The other larger tick would be spread over us and thus keep us warm. Mother and dad and the little baby, who died of exposure shortly after we started out on the trip, had another set of feather ticks for themselves. After baby Sigmund died, I again was the youngest in the family, being six years old.

For our food supply, too, we must give mother credit, for as soon as rumors had reached her that we may have to leave home, she made great preparation. She would bake bread, dry it crisp-dry, and pack it in boxes and little bags. Likewise, father butchered pigs and would cure the meat and pack it in little barrels. Thus we were supplied with food for three months on our way.

In about a month from the time we had left our home we arrived in the first city called "Brobrinsk." Now we thought our troubles were over, for we surely expected to be moved from here by train to Siberia. However, this was not the case. We again had to move by means of the farmer's horse and wagon. We were not at all anxious to get to Siberia, but we were longing to get under some roof and get dried up and washed up and live like human beings. This, however, was only a fancy dream. We had thought that the first months were hard on us, but we discovered that our past suffering was not to be compared to what we had to go through in the future. Most of us became sick; many people among the refugees died every day all around us. Moreover, they were not even given much of a chance to bury their dead, but were pushed on their way. The snow covered the ground and us alike, yet we had to sleep outdoors. Instead of wagons our transportation continued on sleighs for another six weeks, after which we finally reached another city called "Hamel." Here we were unloaded outside the city and it looked to us as if we were forgotten. For many days we sat on the snow-covered ground, huddled up in whatever blankets we could find. At last they put us in the freight train boxcar and we were on our way again facing Siberia. Oh Russia, dark Russia, the land of tears! If all those tears could have risen in clouds that were shed in Russia, perhaps there could be a shower of rain lasting a day.

After traveling along for a few days, our train was pushed on some side road out of their way and apparently forgotten. This was continued many times over. The only account for it was that thereby they thinned the refugees out considerably, for daily there was a death toll, and when we finally reached Siberia our company was not too large for them to house.

The next city where we were again unloaded and numbered was "Kursk." Here we were put into a large building, crowding it full of refugees to such an extent that there was no walking place reserved. The floor at night was covered to the inch with people lying jammed together, almost on top of the other. This seemed mercy to begin with to be permitted to be inside, but oh, how cruel the end! We poor folks who for over two months have had the sky for our ceiling were not physically fit to be jammed together in a house. Sickness and disease took dominion in that room. A sickness by the name of "dysentery" broke upon us and soon our company was thinned out sufficiently so that the trains could handle us again. It was, and still is, astonishing where Russia would get all the refugees. Their railroad system is simply insufficient to handle them all. Thousands and millions have been driven to Siberia during the Czar time. Some were by foot chained together and driven away by horsemen; others were hauled out by wagons and sleighs and the trains ran daily, loaded with criminals going to Siberia. And yet, even at this day of 1947, we find more in the Siberian slave camp than at any other time during the Czar's regime.

Here in the city of "Kursk" the government put before the remaining refugees a proposition. We either could choose to stay there and work for the government in the logging camps, or, if we refused to work for them as slaves, we would be sent on to Siberia. The ones who did remain were the more fortunate ones, for when the revolution broke out; they were the first to get back to their old homes. However, not knowing these things, a great number of them rather preferred to go on to Siberia, among which we were numbered. Father said "I will not work as a slave for them, seeing I have not done anything against the government." So there we were again on our trip to Siberia.

Our next stop was "Waronish," deep in central Russia. Here we were again put off on a side track and forgotten. A great snowstorm drifted our train with heavy snowbanks all around, so when they finally decided to get us on our way, the refugee men had to shovel snow for about a day or more to clear the way.

Our next stop was the city of "Pensa." To our great surprise, the train passed through the city without pushing us to a side track for a few days, as their custom was. But alas! But so very far out of town there was a little village and here was where our train stopped again. Now, we thought, our journey was at an end. Again we were disappointed. Here we were taken from the train and put in some buildings (barracks). Somehow this worked out better for us. God's Word says, "And we know that all things work together for good to them that love God, to them who are the called according to His purpose." (Romans 8:28).

Mother got very sick. We were given permission to take her to the hospital, where she was in bed for six weeks. A baby boy was born here and died in but two or three days. Mother's life was almost taken, too. If you, my dear reader, are a mother, you will understand what my poor mother had to go through in those six weeks.

The rest of our friends were demanded to be on their way, while our family was permitted to remain until mother got out of bed. No sooner was she up than the orders came again to get on our way. We would have gladly remained there if that would have been granted. By that time we were at least a thousand miles from our old beloved home and being so far from the war zone made traveling more easy. In a short time we passed through the city "Samara." This city is located by the famous river "Volga." We crossed this river via the largest bridge in Russia. However, we were not permitted to see it. The conductors came and sealed our door, and in the freight boxcar there are no windows. You must remember that all during this trip on the train we were hauled like cattle in a boxcar. The only light we ever could get was through the door, if we could stand the cold to have it open a crack.

Our next stop was the city "Orenburg." This city is located on the line of Siberia and central Russia. It is built on a very beautiful spot. On one side flows the river "Volga," while on the other side eastward is the river "Ural" and towards the south, some miles away, we find the river "Sokmahr." The population at that time was some 200,000.

Arriving there we were ordered to leave the train and were loaded on sleighs and taken to the deserted army barracks on the outskirts of the city. We had caught up with all our old friends which had to leave while mother was sick. This was a dreadful existence. These barracks were so filled that a person could not even walk through them without stepping over somebody's feet or body. Sickness was raging; death was at work. People counted the dead more fortunate than the living. Who could count all the tears that were shed in those dark barracks? If the walls could have talked they would have told a gruesome, heart-rending story. It was a life full of woe. Being undernourished, we were an easy prey for different diseases.

In scripture we read: "But pray ye that your flight be not in the winter, neither on the Sabbath day." (Matthew 24:20). How well this scripture fitted our situation. Had it been in the summer it would not have been so bad. But here we were in the middle of November, and how cold it appeared to us being plucked out of a nice warm climate as we have it in the beautiful Urkaine. In contrast to this we now were in a country where the thermometer would go down to 65 and 70 below zero in the winter. Besides, there was but a very limited heating system in those barracks. In this climate as described we were held for about a month. It was here in the city of Orenburg where all the refugees were appointed to their final place and punishments.

When our turn came for further transportation, we were ordered to go to the Provence of "Orsk," some 300 miles farther into Siberia. We finally reached our so-called destination in the exile of Siberia on the 20th day of December 1914, in a little village in the Province of Orsk called "Malshanowka."

When I look back over this road of tears, I wonder greatly, even now, from where we had all the strength to withstand all the hardships. Here is the mystery. As God had said to His people of old "When thou passest through the waters, I will be with thee; and through the rivers, they shall not overflow thee: when thou walkest through the fire, thou shalt not be burned; neither shall the flame kindle upon thee. For I am the LORD thy God, the Holy One of Israel, thy Saviour:..." (Isaiah 43:2-3).

CHAPTER III

Our Life In Exile

Ever since the conquest of Siberia by Russia, the government had been sending her criminals into this wild uninhabited country. As soon as the criminals had served their term, and were accustomed to the climate, they were then given an opportunity to become farmers in this country. The government would give them land free of charge and perhaps a little help for a start. Thus, this country became populated by the so-called criminals.

Siberia, at least the eastern part of it, is a good farming country, although the summers are very short and the winters long and cold. The thermometer will go down to about 70 or 75 below zero and usually a good snow blizzard with it. If you are found out-of-doors with not much clothing on, you do feel chilly. In spite of this you can grow a fine crop of grain.

During the Czar's reign Siberia was thrown open for settlement in the same manner as homesteads in America. Many Russians, therefore, who had no land of their own in the civilized countries, would immigrate to Siberia. Likewise, many German-speaking people coming from overcrowded Germany would move to Siberia. So you see, Siberia had a rather mixed population, not only of white races of people, but also a great number of Nomadic tribes who lived all through Siberia.

The homes of these people were built half buried in the ground. The walls were thick and constructed out of clay mingled with straw, and when finished would be perhaps two or three feet thick. The roofs were all thatched. The windows were very small and up near the ceiling when looking from the inside, whereas, from the outside, the windows would be next to the ground. The doors would always open to the inside. The reason for this was because of the snow storms. These snow storms sometimes covered the village completely and in this case, a person could always get out of his house. Inside the house you would find only one room. That is, there would be no partition of any kind in it. As for furniture, there would be one table, its size according to the size of the family in the house. A long bench would be found along the walls for seating accommodations. In one corner of the house you would see a large Russian oven (peatch) made out of bricks and occupying about one-fourth of the entire room. This peatch served as the bed for the entire family from granddad to grandchild. The top of it was always good and warm, so no one had need of any blankets. You would just toast one side at a time, and, of course, keep nice and warm. This is the customary method of sleeping accommodations over all Russia.

These ovens, of course, are also the main and only means for cooking facilities. All the Russian meals are cooked in the oven either in the open flame or after it is hot enough inside to roast or bake anything wanted. The food mainly consists of soup known as "borsht." This is a vegetable soup and is served on the table in one large bowl. Each member of the family has a wooden spoon which makes up the entire cutlery needed in the house.

Not being used to this type of life, you can imagine our surprise when we arrived at this, our appointed place of abode. We never before had seen houses covered with snow. Neither did we before have to sleep on top of a hot stove or oven, nor did ye know how to handle those large wooden spoons. Neither did mother know how to prepare a meal in this nature. All was new. It will be of interest to you to know that the main fuel to heat these monstrous ovens was straw and artificial peat made out of manure and buffalo chips gathered in the pastures during the summer time. The teamster who had the undertaking of delivering us to our new home found it quite a job to explain to us all these new methods.

However, I rejoice to say that we found these Russian people living in Siberia to be of very kind heart. They indeed tried their very best to make it comfortable for us. Many fine food gifts were given to us during the winter.

Father asked permission to remodel the inside of the house somewhat in order to have a little privacy, and this was gladly granted. When they discovered that father was a carpenter, they flooded him with jobs and orders. Likewise with mother, when they discovered that she was a seamstress, orders came in faster than she could handle them. In but a little while our house was a regular workshop, one-half a cabinet maker shop and the other half a tailor shop.

We indeed were thankful to our Lord Jesus Christ who had His merciful hand upon us. We now had the privilege of having a peaceful Christmas holiday in a nice warm house underneath the snow banks.

In this village lived a wealthy man. He owned a large farm and also a nice big house. He lived there only in the winter time because his health demanded a dry cold winter. This man came to father, asking him if he would take over the management of his farm. Father, of course, accepted this offer. We were also permitted to live in this lovely home during their absence.

While father ran the farm, we children took the job of herding the sheep and goats for the whole village. This, of course, was not hard work, and yet a well-paying job. In the fall when our boss and his wife came back, we again moved back to our old quarters. My sister Olga, however, stayed there as their maid.

In the winter of 1915-1916 we lived quite comfortably. We owned a goat to take care of our milk supply, a few chickens, and a cat, which made up our entire earthly possessions. Good as it was, it was not home sweet home. The longing to return to our old home in White Russia was still in our hearts. So in the spring of 1916, father went to the nearest government seat in order to obtain the necessary papers for our return. This was finally granted, because the German front had been pushed back so far by the Russian armies that there was no longer any danger of invasion in the Ukraine and White Russia.

We sold everything we had, with the exception of the things we had brought along with us from home. Among these things was mother's lovely sewing machine of which she thought so much. Here in packing our things a great mistake was made. All our things were packed into heavy bulky packages or boxes, particularly the sewing machine. It was first filled between the legs with books and literature, and then it was wrapped with long rolls of homemade linen. (You may wonder where we got all the rolls of linen.) Well, in Russia during those days practically all the cloth among the poorer class of people was made of flax straw. As you know, the flax has this fiber around the stems. Mother used this to make rolls of fine linen cloth fit to make lovely dresses or suits for children.

We were not very far on our way homeward bound when we learned that our packages were too heavy for father alone to lift around into freight train cars.

CHAPTER IV

Father's Death

It was on the 8th of May, 1916, when we once more boarded a train at the nearest railway station. At the first station we had sufficient help with the loading of our baggage, but when the conductor told us that at the next station we must change trains, we were troubled in mind how we would manage, for there was no one in our family that was of any help when it came to lifting except father, and he had been a ruptured man for many years. On our trip to Siberia we always had sufficient help, as there were many refugees with us, but on the trip back each one was for themselves.

In due time we arrived at the next station, where the conductor gave us a lift in the unloading of the things, but when it came to loading them again, father was left by himself. While father was busy with the work of loading, the trains, of course, were maneuvering back and forth to which we paid little attention. All at once a locomotive pushed some more cars to be hooked on to the train in which we were loading our stuff. Just then father was lifting the heavy sewing machine to the car. This struck his load, breaking him backwards, and alas, the damage was done. Father was internally hurt. He laid down telling us that he was finished. Imagine what a shock that was to us. We stood around him trying to be of help to him, but what could we do? He commenced to swell all over his body. We could see that he had to be taken to the hospital and immediately. So when the train stopped at the nearest large city, which happened to be the city of Orenburg, we all left the train, unloading our stuff with the intentions of staying there until father would recover, should that be God's will. Mother somehow got him to the hospital where he was examined by the doctor. The report was not very good, I can assure you.

Dear reader, can you picture our grief? We children, all young – the oldest only 16 years, mother a very frail little woman, father on his death bed, and here we were in a strange country among strange people. I can assure you that mother was much in prayer in those days, looking to God for help.

We were a little acquainted with the city of Orenburg from our previous stay there when we lived in the barracks on our way to Siberia, as you will recall having read in the chapter before. Since our father was in the hospital, it became necessary for us to make our abode there. We found a little house in the suburbs of the city which we rented to be our home until we would see what the future had in store for us. The accident of father's had happened on a Tuesday. The next day, Wednesday, one of my sisters went to see him and brought a good report home. On Friday another of us went to see him and still the same report. On that following Sunday we all were on our way to the hospital. We purchased some things to cheer him with. As we arrived there, all of us went in and inquired for his room, but oh, the blow when we were told "Mr. Hausmann is dead and buried." Mere words would fail to describe how we felt. We children all broke out crying; mother fainted. This new burden was more than she could bear. We inquired where he was buried, but we were told that these were Revolution days and he was buried like all the rest of them were buried. That meant that he was buried in one of those union graves. A union grave is one large grave where all the dead ones are piled in, head over heels, without clothing or anything in the line of respect but just like old rubbish. Some of those graves had hundreds of dead bodies in them. My own beloved father was one of those who filled the grave. It is indeed horrible to be thrown into a union grave, but that is not the worst. It indeed is much worse to go to a Christless grave! It grieves me to say that my father during his lifetime had shut out Christ. Not that he did not know better, but he just put it off like so many thousands of people do today. Let me tell you God's Word says, "He that being often reproved hardeneth his neck, shall suddenly be destroyed, and that without remedy." (Proverbs 29:1). Again we read "Boast not thyself of to morrow; for thou knowest not what a day may bring forth." (Proverbs 27:1). Let this be a warning to you if you do not know the Lord Jesus Christ as your own personal Savior.

There is a hope in my heart that I might see my father in heaven. Not because I would compromise as to say that a person without being born again could ever get to heaven. No indeed. "Except a man be born again, he cannot see the kingdom of God." (John 3:3). Here is the reason for my hope. The night before father died my brother went to the hospital to see him. Coming back he told us this wonderful news. "When I entered father's room, I found him on his knees beside his bed praying." Well my friends, let me tell you, if that man bent his knees in the hour of death, he must have been saved like the thief on the cross. And no doubt he was saved in answer to mother's prayers, for God's Word tells us that the prayer of a righteous man availeth much, and I know that mother most earnestly prayed for him. Yes, beloved, God must answer the prayers of His children, for such is His promise. (John 14:13).

Two weeks went by and we began to realize that this life of brooding over our sorrow was not helping us any. Besides, the money we had was running low. The rent of the house had to be paid. Every bit of food had to be purchased in the city. Mother could not find enough to sew so as to support us all. As for us children, we thought we were too young to earn any money for support, but God showed us a way. My oldest sister, Adina, found a job in a restaurant as a waitress. Shortly after, my second oldest sister, Olga, went to work in the same restaurant. Later, even sister Herta was given a job by the same boss in the same restaurant because he took a liking to the way the girls worked for him.

When brother Fredrick and I saw that the girls were earning money, we, too, became ambitions. We asked mother for some money to give us a start to become newspaper boys. We earned enough the first day to pay mother back what she had loaned us. At this time only my younger sister, Mathilda, who was then eleven years old, was not earning anything. I recall teasing her about this. However, this was not for very long. Then she, too, was earning her share.

The Russian people are very fond of sunflower seeds. They roast them and eat them in the same manner as we folks in this country eat peanuts. You can at any time in the year buy these seeds at practically every corner of the street in a city, so Mathilda and Mother went to the country and bought from some farmer a bag full of these raw seeds. They dried them very nicely and sold them per glass to the passersby on the street. Thus, she, too, had a nice job to help earn our daily bread.

This type of life in my early childhood days gave me boldness by which I benefitted all my life. Every night after a busy day we children would hand over all our earnings to mother. Each one of us was, of course, trying to be able to hand in the most. Sometimes it was not easy to sell any newspapers during this time of turmoil in the land. I recall going after people until they would buy to get rid of me. I would stop at a street corner and holler out the heading of my newspaper so loud that people could not hear anything but me. Some would buy a paper to keep me silent for a while.

But as time went on, Fredrick and I were not satisfied

with our job. We started something else. We rented a little stall in the open air marketplace and began selling such things as toys, straw hats, hairpins, collar pins, and the like. We also had sort of a gambling machine going. Men would play a game on it. It was just a round board with sixty holes in it. In the center there was a tall stern where marbles were thrown. They would roll through and lodge in these holes, and the person reaching the highest number won the game. We, of course, would only charge so much per game. This proved to us boys a good money-making machine.

This type of work we carried on under the most difficult circumstances, for in those days of Revolution in the land money was not worth much. There was all kinds of money in the land because of the different parties ruling the country and each party would have its own money. Only that money of the party holding the upper hand at the front line in the war zone would be considered good. There were five different parties. That meant five different governments and five different types of money to watch according to the war procedure day by day.

Next to these difficulties, we were always in danger of being attacked by some bullies who like to take advantage over the smaller. It was quite common for us to come home with a bleeding head or limping leg. In those days you had to fight to live. I used to carry in one of my pant-legs a solid rubber hose with which I would fight the fellows attacking me. Sometimes we would fight to kill until someone came to the rescue. Such were my childhood days. One night I was attacked by a group of boys. They wanted to take my money away. They got hold of me and searched me for money. I used to carry my money in a little slip bag around my neck and then tucked it through my shirt collar against my bare body. This these boys knew. They got hold of me and were trying to cut the string around my neck with a jack-knife. I was not so sure, if, at the same time, they did not also plan to cut my neck. Let me assure you, I fought, and the good Lord helping me, I got away from them.

Shortly after this, while walking through the city late one night; I felt a whip wind itself around my bare legs. I wore short pants in those days, only being nine years old. Another time I came to, when a man lifted me up and told me that my head was bleeding. Someone had thrown a rock against my head and knocked me out. I do not know for how long, but this kind gentleman took me home when I told him my address. Such were my childhood days. Fight for your life every day and every step of your way.

CHAPTER V

The Revolution

Permit me to take you back one year to the year of 1917. This was the year after the death of my father. This was the year when Russia was plunged into a Civil War led by the revolutionist "Lenin."

The parties that were engaged in this upheaval were as follows: Bolsheviks (which is in Soviet Union now) the Kosaks, (who were the Czar's armies), Kerenskey, Petlurtzy, and Machnowtzy. These five parties each were fighting for supremacy or rulership over Russia. Those were the days when life was cheap. Blood was flowing freely. The human heart which the Prophet Jeremiah describes as being "Deceitful above all things and desperately wicked: who can know it?" (Jeremiah 17:9) was then revealed before us to be even so and worse.

In and around the cities of Orenburg, Samara, and Buzzuluk, where most of the fighting took place, the Bolsheviks, and Kosaks were strongly represented, since this is where a lot of the Volga Kosaks lived. The other three parties were present, but not so forcefully. In two years, that is 1917 and 1918, I personally witnessed the city of Orenburg to be five times under war raid and invasion back and forth between Bolsheviks and Kosaks. Each time one party conquered above the other, the conquering one would revenge against their enemies in utter destruction. Men, women and children, all that were thought to be of the other party would be killed off and their homes set on fire. Then again when they had to flee, if the other party would get too strong for them, they would set fire to all granaries or any type of food supply in order not to leave it to their enemies. This was carried on back and forth five times, each of the parties trying to be a little more cruel than the one before them.

My dear reader, if I were to paint a picture of a revolution, I would choose the blackest paint on earth and then I must frankly admit that I could not paint it black enough. The things that I have seen and taken notice of are not lawful to mention among people. If you are prepared to listen to gruesome things, here are some things that went on at that time:

They would take the people who were to be killed and drive them into a house, bar and lock every door and window and then massacre them with knives. The women folks they would rip open. I personally saw little ones lying beside their mothers which were never born, but just gushed out because its mother had been ripped open. Some women folks were filled with bottles, and then smashed inside them. From some men they would rip strips of skin off their backs in different ways, as Satan directed them. I personally saw human bodies lying chopped asunder, ripped asunder, and arms and legs and heads scattered around on the street. At cemeteries you could see human bodies piled up like heaps of wood. No wonder God's Word tells us that "The heart is deceitful above all things and desperately wicked: who can know it?"

During those days mother would take us children down to the cellar where we all would kneel down, and she between us, would spread her arms over us and pray. As long as mother prayed we youngsters would feel quite safe. I thank God for a praying mother.

In God's Word we read: "Samaria shall become desolate; for she hath rebelled against her God: they shall fall by the sword; their infants shall be dashed in pieces, and their women with child shall be ripped up." (Hosea 13:16).

These things I have seen with my own eyes come to pass. Only one-third of the population of a city of 200,000 was left alive; the rest fell by the sword. You might say: Of course, only Russia would do such things. We in America would never become so wicked. We are much more civilized, you know! Let me assure you beloved, that if a revolution should break out, those very things would go on in America. If the law of the country is removed and there is no more fear of punishment, if all the criminals in our penitentiaries are turned loose with the privilege of doing as they please, America would be flooded with blood in no time. Moreover, if a revolution breaks out, the people who now live peacefully, but have no use for God, are filled with satanic thirst for blood.

After the Revolution, when the Bolsheviks had the upper hand, came what they called purging. They began to purge the country from all those that they thought were their enemies or spies. Beloved, I could write a book on this alone, but I shall take it very briefly.

Great numbers were gathered together and driven to the cemetery, where they were stripped of all their clothing. Then they had to dig their own graves. The weaker ones were shot into them and the stronger ones had to shovel earth on them. Then the stronger ones were put up, too, and done away with in the same manner. Thus it continued day after day until a person was afraid that all living in the city would have to face the same end. The boss of the restaurant where my sisters worked, one of the finest men you could look for on earth, was among those who had to dig his own grave. He was suspected of being rich, and no rich folks were permitted to live in those days. Even farmers who had a decent farm and were not exactly in rags were numbered among the (Burzhooy) rich and, of course, had no right to live. These were the days when the beggars, the drunkards, the gamblers, the criminals, and all the lower and base class of people had the right to live and tell others when and how they wanted them to die.

In 1918, after things had calmed down a little, we once again attempted to go on our trip homeward to White

Russia. We really longed to get home. We got rid of practically all our goods, including the sewing machine, which was directly responsible for the death of father.

Being on our way, we came some hundred miles nearer home into a little city called Buzzuluk. Here, however, we learned that this was as far as we would get, for all the railroads were destroyed by the war and revolution. We sought for a place to settle down, but finding nothing, we just joined the hundreds of other folks, who were in the same fix and made our home under the blue sky. The three older sisters took the train back to Orenburg where they got their jobs back again. Mother, Fredrick, Mathilda, and I stayed at Buzzuluk. After a long search for living quarters, we found an empty storehouse which used to be, some years back, a storage house for an old four mill. We moved into it, cornered off a little corner, and made a stove out of clay and beds out of old boards we found lying around.

My brother went as an apprentice in a shoemaker's shop. The master was a well-known man by the name of Adolf Kuhn, of whom you will read much in this book later on.

This life in the old storage house was indeed a very trying winter for us. Money was very scarce. Our wood, just branches, had to be carried on our backs for about three or four miles, and then we had to cross a river (a little branch of the Volga). Sometimes the water would be up to our belts and over, for there was no bridge. Next to this chore we would have to be busy every day trying to earn a little money for food. Mother and I would walk to the villages and buy eggs from the farmers. We took them home and boiled them, after which we would take them to the railroad station and sell them to the soldiers. Most of the soldiers in Russia had no money, so they would trade us herring for eggs. That was the main food fed to the soldiers, and, of course, they were tired of herring. We, in turn, could sell these herrings on the market and so we traded with them. Thus mother and I were active every day trading and selling whatever we could in order to sustain our lives. This, of course, was only possible because the good Lord was with us, for during that time people were starving in the town and everywhere for lack of food.

However, we managed to go through that summer, fall, and part of winter, when the hardest days of all my days on earth were ahead of me. I shall find it hard to write the next chapter, for this chapter to follow will relate to you the greatest loss in my life.

CHAPTER VI

The Greatest Loss in My Life

It is bad enough when a nation fights another nation. It is much worse when a country has to go through a revolution. But that is nothing to be compared with when a nation has to go through a period of raging famine in their country. This was the case in the years 1919 and 1920 in the eastern parts of Russia.

We lived at that time, as you recall from the chapter before, in the little city called Buzzuluk in the Providence of Samara. This Province, as well as the province of Orenburg, was very much exhausted in food and other necessities of life due to two years of revolution the country had just gone through. In addition to the revolution we had the grasshopper epidemic and also an unusual drought sweeping through the entire eastern parts of Russia. All the previous trials with the in-creeping starvation had weakened the people to such an extent that there was no resistance left to fight the different epidemics of diseases which were sweeping over the country. You can always look for all sorts of diseases to come upon the nation after a war or revolution.

The first epidemic that swept the country was malaria. This was brought in by the refugees which had fled from the warmer parts of Russia known as "Tashkant" because of a raging famine in that part of Russia. Many people fell victim to the malaria fever, seeing that it is a contagious disease. I, too, was one of the many victims. Should you not be acquainted with the symptoms of malaria, I will say a few words to introduce you to it. There are these two extremes active in your body – the extreme cold and the extreme heat. When you are attacked you would think the only comfortable place you could find is in a hot oven, as every member of your body is at a freezing point. Again the other extreme after the cold is the burning up in your body, and you long to find a place where to cool your parched tongue and your burning limbs and body.

Before the epidemic was over another followed which was even worse, namely typhus fever. Now this is a dreadfull disease, indeed. I personally believe that more people fell victim to typhus than to any other disease that had struck the country until that time. There was hardly a home where the death angel had not visited. Every member in our family was also stricken down with it. I personally had not yet recovered from malaria when typhus struck me down. How I ever survived is beyond me. Likewise, my brother and sister had it and also recovered from it. I don't think there could have been a harder time that poor mother ever experienced in all her days of life. Here we were, all three in bed, and the oldest ones away in Orenburg, working to keep alive. There was hardly any food in the house nor in the country and we had no fuel. She had to carry the wood on her back about three or four miles and she was just a fragile little woman without nourishing food to sustain her and the winter was hard with much snow to contend with. After about two months of struggling in this nature, we youngsters were again able to get up and be of a little help, but oh, so little. I remember my legs would tremble if I stood up; likewise were my brother's and sister's legs.

We had no sooner recovered and were of some help to Mother when she took ill with the same disease. I can only too well recall the intense suffering that she had to go through and we were not in any position to help her much, being left very weak ourselves, and having no money or product with which to help a sick person. I went around from house to house begging for bread and foodstuffs.

My brother, having learned how to fix shoes, hung out a sign saying, "Shoe Repairer," and thus he would make a few (kopeeks) cents, as the people who still had some money would get their shoes fixed. We did very much to try to do our best to supply poor mother with some nourishing things. The sisters from Orenburg would, off and on, send us some little help, too. Thus week after week went by, with no visible result of improvement, but rather growing weaker and weaker. We began to realize the dreadful situation when she finally lost her voice. We sent a message to our sisters in Orenburg to come home if at all possible, but the answer came back that they were unable to come due to the poverty there. Finally came the night that caused me the greatest pain and sorrow that I have ever been called upon to endure.

To picture this scene in mere words is far from adequate to describe it. The grief and agony which we passed through on that most horrible night is to me beyond words. Oh, that it were only a dream, but no, it was only too true. Picture us three youngsters standing around the bedside of our dear mother, the most precious person in all the world. We did not dare to think of living without mother. There she lay, hovering between life and death. I am sure that it pained her much more than even us to think of leaving her helpless children in a cold, cruel, starving world. Yet her hour had come to leave. It was hard to believe at that time that "...all things work together for good to them that love God, to them who are called according to his purpose." (Romans 8:28). Mother had committed us to the keeping of the Great Heavenly Father, for we had no earthly father to look to for sustenance. She had told me before she lost her voice that she had dedicated me to the Lord at the day of my birth and she often told me that it was her wish that if I grew up to manhood I should be a minister of the gospel or a missionary.

Here she lay grappling with the last enemy, "the enemy, death." We felt so helpless; nothing that we could say or do would stay the hand of the grim reaper nor bring relief to that burning fever. We realized only too well that death was coming nearer and nearer. It was a cold dark night outside as well as within. The surroundings were most grim, dismal and cheerless. In addition to our present grief and sorrow, starvation was staring us in the face. The thought of facing a cold winter without mother was unbearable. Our dwelling place was only an old abandoned warehouse where rats and mice held full possession. We two boys managed to partition off one corner where we had living quarters. Our furniture consisted of a cook-stove which we had made from old bricks and clay, a few rough boards nailed together on some wobbly legs which served as a table, and a few wooden benches that served as chairs. A small window in one wall furnished the lighting system. Our beds were constructed from some old boards lying around there with straw for a mattress. This we called home for more than two years. In addition to this it also served as a workshop for my brother Fredrick who was engaged in repairing shoes to make a few pennies. My sister, Mathilda, did her best to keep house for the family and nurse mother as well. I, being the youngest of the three, acted as general roustabout boy, carrying water and fuel.

At this time Fredrick was 16 years old, Mathilda was 13, and I was 11. Terrified and grief-stricken, we huddled together and spent the night praying and crying and trying to cheer one another that mother will yet be spared for us. There was no light in the house; we had no lamp nor kerosene. The only light we could produce was by lighting kindling and holding them in our hands as torches. Thus we stood around the bed of our dying mother.

It was about two o'clock in the morning when we

noticed a change coming over her face. She made an effort to speak, but her voice was gone. We were not able to catch any words but understand that she was bidding us farewell and God bless you. She gave us such a searching look. I shall never forget that look. I am certain that was just another expression of her wish that we should look to Jesus for our help. We also knew that the last breath of her life here on earth was a prayer. She closed her eyes and lay quiet for a moment, then opened them again just to look us over once more and then she went to be with the Lord where there shall be no more pain, sorrow, sickness, nor death.

There we stood, three orphans, cast upon the mercies of God to Whom mother faithfully had committed us. For a while we just gave way to our feelings. Brother laid the body of mother straight, then we embraced each other in the dark and let the tears flow freely. Mathilda became hysterical and seemingly could not quit crying. Fredrick and I tried to be brave and comfort her as best we knew how. In spite of our deep sorrow there seemed to be One with us, even the Lord Jesus Christ, whose presence was felt. He alone could speak to our broken hearts as He spoke to Mary and Martha of old, "I am the resurrection, and the life: he that believeth in me, though he were dead, yet shall he live." (John 11:25). Oh, to have had a praying mother.

Dear reader, do you have a praying mother? If you do, you have the most precious heritage on this side of eternity. You should get down on your knees and thank the Lord for her. You may shake off a sermon preached by the best preacher in the world, or you may run away from the best instruction ever received, but you will never run away or shake off the prayers of a godly mother.

Now before starting on the next chapter, may I ask a question of you, mother or father, if it is you who are reading this. Are you praying for your children? Remember you owe them something that shall lead them to the path of righteousness. God holds you responsible for their knowledge of Him. The child will look to his parents for an example. What will you answer at the judgment bar if the child to whom you gave birth will point his finger at you and accuse you of not having told him or her of the way of salvation? I believe the worst pain in eternal hell will be when children whom we bought into this world will charge us before God for not having told them the way of salvation.

I believe the precious name "mother" is too sweet to give to a woman that does not pray for her children. I really think it is an awful sin for women to lead their children through life without prayer, and the name "Mother" is too precious to give to a cigarette smoking, ungodly woman of our age.

I do thank God for having been born of a godly mother, and it is only because of her prayers that I am what I am today. I am today a minister of the precious Gospel of our Lord Jesus Christ, as according to her covenant made with Him at the day of my birth.

CHAPTER VII

Life Without Parents

After the funeral of our beloved mother we felt rather lost in the old warehouse. Besides that, our sister, Mathilda, was so very much afraid to stay in this place after the death of mother that every time she had to walk through the porch where there were no windows (light) one of us boys had to be with her, holding her hand. For a while we had to live with some people we knew in the city; however, this could not be carried on for very long because somehow we had to try to make our own living.

We again went back to our old home, the warehouse. We tried to do some cleaning up in order that Fredrick could resume his work as shoe repairer, as this was our only means of income. During this effort of getting settled new trouble set in. When we washed the bedding upon which mother had died, Mathilda, being run down and frightened, broke down, being reminded of that dreadful night. She had to go to bed and apparently had an attack of typhus fever the second time. For several weeks she was in bed between life and death. Many times we boys gave her up. However, God somehow saw it fit to keep her alive. How she could keep alive I don't understand, for we did not have anything in the house to nourish a sick person with; in fact, there was not sufficient food to keep a well person alive.

One day we were visited by Mr. Adolf Kuhn, of whom you have read about in the previous chapters. The Lord put into his heart to take pity on the poor little girl. He therefore, of his own accord, took our little sick girl and took her to Orenburg to her older sisters, where she received better care.

We two boys, Fredrick and I, remained alone. Fredrick

was busy in shoe repairing; whereas, I became his housekeeper, such as you may expect from a 12 year old boy. Before long things seemed to improve a little. Summer had come and the poorer folks somehow revived with it. I was helping my brother a little with shoe repairing work and at times when food failed, I would go to the more wealthier people in the city and beg for food. Thus I would go from house to house begging bread.

If you never experienced or lived where there is a famine, you would not understand how it is when I said that people were dying from hunger and then at the other place I said I went begging among the wealthier people. Well, a famine never rages among people that have sufficient money to buy food at high cost. The poorer class of people would be dying on the streets perhaps by the dozens; whereas, the rich people would never as yet miss a meal. At many places you would find some living in luxury; whereas, others died for want of food. Such is the world full of injustice and unrighteousness of men who do not care about others, but only care for themselves and their selfish gain

During this time we boys somehow longed to have one of our four lovely sisters with us. We longed for someone to cook our meals and wash our clothes. By this time we had become so filthy there was not a clean pair of underwear nor shirt to be found in the house, not saying anything of the bedding. Even though we boys did wash every week or so, it seemed impossible to get things clean. Next to dirt our clothes became a real hatchery for lice and fleas. Without exaggeration I could just reach into my bosom and bring them out without looking for them. It was high time indeed for a thorough cleanup, such as only a woman could promote.

We wrote to our sisters and begged them that one of them would take pity on us poor boys and come to help us out of this consuming mess. After much begging and persuasion, one came. It was Olga, our second oldest sister. This summer seemed to go along fine, though you would not call it living in comparison to the American life, but we thought it was living royally in comparison to the days behind us. It was very surprising to us what a feminine touch could do in an old shack or warehouse. In no time we were clean from the lice problem. Likewise, delicious meals out of the meager providence that Fredrick brought in were set before us, reminding us of motherly care.

During this time a mighty spiritual revival broke out in the country. Many of those poor Russians which had been held under the darkness of the Greek Catholic Church came to the marvelous light of salvation through the blood of Jesus Christ. Olga and Fredrick were saved and were baptized during that summer. Oh, the joy you could see in the life of these Russians who saw the light. These poor people never did have a chance in Russia. Ever since Russia became civilized as a nation the entire country was held under the darkness of Greek Catholicism. When spiritual light broke through to some of them they really took it earnestly in talking to others about it. They would stand on the street corner and stop the passersby and ask them personally if they knew Jesus as their personal Saviour. The ungodly government would punish and beat them, but that did not stop them from testifying for Christ.

My beloved reader, if you are not a born again believer in Christ, you then will not be able to understand this above paragraph. If you have accepted Christ as your own personal Saviour and have passed from death unto life, you will know about the joy I am talking about. You then will understand what it meant to those poor Russian folks who had been held in darkness of sin and now at last saw the marvelous Light of Salvation.

It was during this summer that Mr. Adolf Kuhn became very friendly to our cook, Olga. The result of this friendship brought it to pass that we poor fellows lost our sister when she one day became Mrs. Adolf Kuhn. In a way we were pleased to have Adolf as our brother-in-law, but indeed we were sorry to lose Olga, who at the time was to us like a mother.

So there we were, two helpless boys, again trying to live the best we knew how.

CHAPTER VIII

Facing Famine in Its Grim Reality

Much hardship and suffering during the time of exile, revolution, loss of father and mother, and sickness has been explained in the previous chapters. However, until the years of 1919 and 1920 I never had faced what is known as a real famine, even though some people had been dying from hunger here and there. In this year the graves opened their months wide to consume famine's victims.

In the summer before, hardly anything had been sown due to the fact that many farmers did not have the seed. The little bit of grain which was to be found here and there among some farmers was precious in their eyes for immediate food. Those few which had sowed in little had received very little in return because of the drought in that particular year. By the time winter set in, food was not to be found anywhere. Even horses, camels, and such unclean animals as dogs and cats were all used for food. The old hides which were stored up for leather were all used for food.

The government could have shipped in food from the Ukraine, where they had it in abundance, but they seemed to be too much taken up with the enforcement of their new law. The main objective of the government in those days was to exterminate Christianity. Anti-religious groups were organized. Authority was given them that all churches should be either destroyed or remodeled. Most of the churches were burned, some were changed to stables, and some changed to theaters. The anti-religious groups were authorized to disturb every kind of religious worship and to arrest people who were in the habit of going to church and to confiscate their food supply if any were to be found. The victims were to be sent to Siberia for hard labor for life.

Many hundreds of thousands of saints of God suffered the supreme sacrifice and thus became martyrs for the Name of Christ.

In one way the new government had reason to strike against religion, because the Russian Greek Catholic State Church had most miserably failed. Russia in all its history never did have a religion that was of any benefit to the country. The whole country was dominated by the state church and all the people were held in darkness, ignorance, and superstition. Ghost belief and witchcraft were just as common as in the heathen countries of Africa and India. The forgiveness of sins by the priest was taught and granted in advance. For instance, if you wanted to beat up on somebody and you were afraid you might kill him and go to hell, you could go to the priest, pay him a good sum of money, and have your sins forgiven. Then in case the person dies under your punishment, you would not be held responsible by God for it. Next to this, drunkenness was tolerated by the Church and practiced by the priests.

Now when the country had freed itself through revolution from the Pope, the Soviet State demanded submission of the Church. Since the government was made up of God-hating men, they did not see the difference between true Christianity and just religion. There were in those days many true Christian churches in Russia of all different denominations who were not recognized by the Czar's government, but the Bolshevik government knew no difference and struck out at all the churches alike. Immediately the apostate churches linked up with the anti-religious regime and cursed God and were therefore extended the right-hand of fellowship by the Communists, whereas the true Christian bodies refused to have friendship. This, of course, reflected upon them as if it were the true Christian church that was anti-government. This brought about a very severe dominion wide Christian persecution in which hundreds of thousands of true believers of Christ became martyrs for their faith in Jesus.

Now during this time of upheaval we two boys, Fredrick and I, were still living in that old warehouse, with which you are well acquainted by now from the chapter before this one. In spite of the fact that we were trying to keep above the starving line it was getting to the place of impossibility. No more money could be earned; moreover, money would not buy food. There were many days when we boys felt the pain of hunger growing in our stomachs. I believe that starving to death is one of the most painful deaths there is in this dying world.

During this time Fredrick reached the age of military service. In those days boys were drafted at the age of sixteen. Somehow, he, being a Christian, did not care to go into the Army. He would not have lived very long. He would either have died spiritually or bodily. One day he told me that if I did not find him I should not be surprised. So it was that one morning I found myself alone. A note was left behind which read "Do not look for me; do not mention my name; try to save your life. I cannot help you. Your brother F" Well, there I was! All alone, no home, no father, no mother, no brother, and no sisters around me, a little boy of 13 years old, half-starved and clothed with rags. I went to my bother in law's place some distance away, but there was no place for me. They were already a family of seven counting Adolf's mother, two sisters, one brother and his wife, and Adolf and Olga.

I then tried to get into the orphanage home, such as it was, but here I was told that only children up to 12 years of age were admitted. I was one year too old. They told me that I would receive a little help if I came around daily. I had no home. That old warehouse was gruesome to me. You may be assured I was not very fearful, but just put yourself in that condition. A little boy of 13 living all alone in a large empty building where rats had dominion and where your own beloved mother had died.

Being anxious of get admission into the orphanage home, I dug up the old birth certificates where all the children born in our family were recorded. I was recorded to have been born in 1906. This however, most probably was not correct, for at the time of exile when we left, father went to the authorities there and requested that a birth certificate would be granted for us children. All eight youngsters were put on one sheet of paper and when father was asked our age, he put us all one year apart. This did not seem quite logical, so I made an eight out of the six, thus making me two years younger according to the certificate. I then presented this document to the orphanage home and was admitted, but God helping me, I soon fled. It was a hell hole. If I would have remained there I would have lost my faith in God, and no doubt would have also lost my earthly life.

They would teach the children from cartoons the most blasphemous things against God you could ever imagine. Such as, in regard to the scripture found in John 6:48+53, where Jesus says, "I am the bread of life...Verily, verily I say unto you, Except ye eat of the flesh of the Son of man, and drink his blood, ye have no life in you." They would present a cartoon with Christ lying on the floor and all the people around Him having a chunk of flesh from His body in their hand, and drinking His blood, and thus polluting the young minds of these children. Many other gruesome Cartoons were also presented.

They would make the children pray to God for food and give them none. Next they would make them pray to Lenin and then give them food, telling the children to curse God, because He does not answer their prayers. Romans 1:21-23 suits them perfectly. "Because that, when they knew God, they glorified him not as God, neither were thankful; but became vain in their imaginations, and their foolish hearts was darkened. Professing themselves to be wise, they became fools, and changed the glory of the uncorruptible God into an image made like to corruptible man, (Lenin) and to birds, and fourfooted beasts, and creeping things." What a picture this is of Soviet Russia.

I did not stick around there very long. It seemed to me I was in the foreground of Hell itself. I left, not knowing whither I went. The only thing I benefitted by in all this was that I became two years younger which perhaps was my right age, after all. So from henceforth my age counts from 1908.

It was no easy task for me just to go around and beg, etc. Those days of suffering, though I did not see it then, were given to me for a definite purpose so that I might gain a rich experience which I now greatly use in my ministry of the Gospel. If you would have seen me in those days, you would not have thought very much of my life – only another little ragged boy awaiting the time when he would be hauled out to the union grave or thrown into the heap where they used to haul out hundreds of them to the outskirts of the city, pile them in heaps, pour kerosene over them, and set them on fire.

My feet were covered with a pair of slippers made out of willow bark. This kind of footwear was very common in Russia. Practically everybody of the poorer class wore willow bark (Laptrees) shoes. I recall one day while walking about the city I saw an old man putting some sort of oil on a camel's skin that had a rash. Camels are very common in Siberia. After he was through, he threw those rags away. Having need of some rags, I picked them up and wrapped them around my feet which were frozen. I thought these oily rags would keep my feet warm, but in a few days I found that I had more than just warm feet. I had contracted the itch which the camel had. This horrible disease broke out between my toes and fingers. All over my body I was a living burning itch. For some time I suffered from this, but somehow it left me without the use of any medicine, of which I had none.

The famine got worse and worse. People were dying everywhere. One day I begged a fellow on the street for a meatball he was frying and selling. He tossed me one and it tasted delicious. The next day that man was arrested for selling human flesh.

There were scores of little fellows like myself roaming around on the streets. We used to form bands and overtake people at the market that were selling food and help ourselves. At night we would crowd into the railroad station to keep warm. In early morning they would come around with a wagon and pick out the dead ones and haul them out to be burned or buried. One day I got on top of a boxcar of a train that was bound for Orenburg. I tried to get to my sisters living at Orenburg. For some time I was lying on the roof but it got too cold, so I slipped down between two cars and straddled the bumper. The Russian trains have a different kind of bumper than do the American boxcars. They have two large plates which come together and over each spring of these plates there is a kind of platform. I would straddle one of these. For miles and hundreds of miles I would sit there, hanging on for dearlife and having these boxcars slam together between my legs until I would literally turn deaf from the noise. Should I have slipped, I would not be here to tell the story.

Arriving at Orenburg, I set out at once to find my sisters. It was a great surprise to them to see me again, having not heard of me for some time. My sister Adina, the oldest sister, got busy right away, and made me a suit out of gunny sacks which she was able to obtain in the restaurant where they worked. There was famine in the city of Orenburg too, but not to such an extent as there was in

Buzzuluk which I had just left. Both of my sisters, Adina and Herta, still held their jobs and Mathilda was with them in their apartment which they held. However, the famine was closing around more and more.

Through the help of Adina and some friends she knew in the country in the collective farms I was able to get a job in a government farm some twelve miles out of Orenburg. My job was to pasture the working horses at night time. This indeed was no hard job. I enjoyed it immensely. The food was good and I began to grow and put on weight and it was no time until I forgot all about the past.

This particular farm went ahead with their spring work, hoping somehow to conquer the famine in their own strength...against God and making light of His love for man. His Word, however, still remains true – "If my people, which are called by my name, shall humble themselves, and pray, and seek my face, and turn from their wicked ways; then will I hear from heaven, and will forgive their sin, and will heal their land." (II Chronicles 7:14). This is just what Russia would not do. They would not humble themselves; neither would they pray. So the Lord gave them dust for rain, desolation instead of vegetation, etc. It was not so very long until this collective farm, like so many others, was left desolate and vacant. Even as we read in the Book of Isaiah when the people would not humble themselves before God, "Your country is desolate, your cities are burned with fire; your land, strangers devour it in your presence..." (Isaiah 1:7).

One by one they pulled out of that collective farm, everything came to an end, and the hopes of harvest as well as the immediate food for the acing stomach were gone. I, too, walked back to the city, hoping to find refuge with my sisters. But what did I find? I found myself in the jaws of death. There in the city was the dreadful deadly disease, cholera. On my way to my sisters I met with many who were groaning in death. People were lying dead in the streets, others dropping with the horrors of death written on their faces. Cholera is a powerful enemy to life. Any person getting it will be dead in 20 or 30 minutes. The symptoms first noticed are these: the face turns bluish black, the stomach throws up everything in it, and the muscles begin to contract to such an extent that the joints in your limbs will jump out of place. The person, not being able to stand it, just passes on screaming in agony of pain. As I stood in the city amongst the dying, I truly was reminded of this portion of the scripture–"Walking through the valley of the shadow of death."

These dead corpses were then gathered up by special carts going about the city for this very purpose and hauled out to the graveyard where they would be buried in mass graves, or the union graves I talked about in the chapter before.

I had been home just a few days when my sister, Adina, took ill with cholera. Herta had heard that if the patient just attacked is rubbed with kerosene the life sometimes can be saved. This was faithfully tried to the best of our knowledge. However, it only prolonged her agony and she died. After the departure of Adina, we three, Herta, Mathilda, and I, were so bowed down with grief that we just sat there and waited for death to lay hold of us next. We did not feel it worthwhile to make an effort against it or try to escape. As a rule when there is one in the family falling victim to this disease the rest shortly follow. This did not prove to be the case with us, or else I would not be here to tell the story.

We called for the young man to whom Adina was engaged to be married, Mr. Roman. He indeed was a heart-broken young fellow when he saw his young bride-to-be cold in death. He refused to have her hauled out with the rest and managed to give her a decent burial. He, himself, made the coffin; as such things were not available in those days. He found someone to take the remains on a cart as it was too heavy for the four of us, Herta, Mathilda, Mr. Roman and I, to carry her. There was no minister to commit the body to the earth, so Mr. Roman himself took matters in hand and performed the funeral committal by reading a portion of scripture. Since he was not a Christian he could not pray, so Herta led in a simple little prayer after which we ourselves had to shovel the earth on our dearly beloved sister. Adina was only 21 years old when she died. No doubt she is with the Lord, having been a Christian from childhood, though I must admit she was in backslidden condition at the time of death.

This was now the third time that my heart was broken when a loved one was lowered to rest; father, mother, and Adina, to whom I looked up to as not only father, mother and sister, but also as the one upon whom I could rely for support and refuge in sorrow.

Before this, you will recall, four little brothers which were all younger than I had already died. At the time they died we felt keenly the loss, but at this time I counted them fortunate and wished that I would have been one of them. However, my lot was to remain alive and to face the cruel life with a determined set jaw to fulfill the blessed covenant my beloved Christian mother had made with her God.

CHAPTER IX

Finding a Haven of Refuge

As I look back upon the things gone through thus far, I cannot help seeing God's protecting hand upon me, for again and again I was saved from certain death. He had led me safely through the valley of the shadow of death where hundreds and perhaps thousands had fallen around me. Not because I was any better or stronger than any of those who fell, but simply because, as I believe, the Lord had promised to my praying dying mother that this son of hers would preach the Gospel.

I told my two sisters that were left, Herta and Mathilda, that I was leaving Orenburg. Of course they did not try to keep me back, as in those days they were not able to help me should I remain with them. Moreover, all the people there felt doomed to die of the cholera epidemic, for by that time over half of the inhabitants of the city had fallen victims.

After saying goodbye for the last time to Herta and Mathilda, I went to the station to see if I could jump a freight train. This was in the month of July, 1920. Due to the warm season of the year I did not mind riding on the roof of a boxcar, if only I would be permitted to stay on it. After loafing around for some time, I saw a train pull out in my direction. I jumped it and was on my way. It was now my intention to keep on going west until I would reach the Ukraine. When I arrived at Buzzuluk I stopped off to see my sister Olga, Mrs. Adolf Kuhn. Coming to their place I was horror stricken as I found their house deserted. My first thought, of course, was that they had died from cholera, for that had been my daily sight and thought all that year in the city of Orenburg.

I inquired around among the neighbors as to what had

become of the "Kuhns." After a long painful search for them I discovered they were alive and had gone to the German Mennonite colonies some hundred miles away from Buzzuluk.

Having suffered much from hunger on my trip from Orenburg, I was busy running from house to house begging food. Now here is a startling thing: As you may realize, this was a famine country. People were dying for want of food, and yet, I would go out begging for food and get it. How could it be done? All I can see, it was the mercy of God who directed me to such homes as He directed Elijah of old, as we read in I Kings 17 where he was directed to the Zarephath widow where the meal in the barrel did not waste and the cruse of oil failed not.

For some time I debated in my mind what to do. Should I go on to the Ukraine or first locate my sister? There was no railroad on which to get to the Mennonite colonies. The only way to get there in my case was walking. After much consideration, I finally felt led of the Lord to locate Olga. I got the directions and set out. However, it appeared to be quite an undertaking for a twelve year old, half-starved boy to start on a hundred mile walk. But since it was the only way, I cast myself upon my mother's God in whose care I was.

When I arrived in the first village out of the city of Buzzuluk I went about again to see if I could get something for my hungry stomach. An old lady in the village gave me a couple of cookies made of dried leaves and grass mingled with some flour. I can assure you they tasted good, too. In fact, in those days, everything tasted good. She directed me to the Greek Catholic priest in the village that would have food. I went to this priest and told him of my condition. He had compassion on me and gave me a good supper and also a place to stay overnight.

The next day I continued again on my journey, being

much strengthened with something in my stomach and lunch on my way. I appeared to be a happy boy. On my way, I was picked up by a man riding horseback. This man was on his way to the market to sell his last horse in order to buy some food for his family. He told me later when we arrived at the market that when he saw me he thought, "That little ragged boy would be better off dead than alive." He said to me, "I had the intention when I picked you up to knock you over the head and put you out of misery, but when you offered me your last piece of bread you had with you; I just could not do it." When I heard that, I was afraid of him and got quickly away. In my heart I knew it was not the bread I gave him that stopped him from knocking me over the head, but rather it was the mighty hand of God that stopped him from the wicked deed.

After being on my journey in like manner for three days, sleeping in old barns or houses or straw stacks or wherever I found a place to rest, I finally reached the first German Mennonite colony. Here I saw that these people were far from starving. They seemed to have all the food they needed. You could see a tremendous difference in these people. They had not tasted famine as yet. "Why this great difference?" you may ask. First, because they feared God; and second, because they knew how to work their land so that it would produce the crop. The difference was so great, as the contrast between the children of Israel and the Egyptians in the days of Moses, or you may say, as light and darkness. You could find people busy harvesting their grain. Threshing machines were being used, whereas I never before had been a threshing machine in Russia, expect on the government farms. This indeed was a surprise to me. Moreover, the trees were all green, whereas in the Russian villages even the trees were all withered up and leaves used for food.

The buildings were larger and painted white and all

were built nicely in a row according to one plan, as if one man had the contract of all the construction. The yards had flower beds, etc. Oh, the joy which flooded my soul when I arrived there. I had indeed passed from death unto life. My thoughts went back to Orenburg. How could I ever make this known to my two dear sisters in the city of death? This was impossible, and even if they would know about it, they could not take a journey as I used to do. The morality was so low in Russia during those days that no young lady could ever dare to go alone. It just was not safe for decent women to go any place.

Having arrived in these colonies, I inquired everywhere if someone had heard of a young couple by the name of Adolf Kuhn moving here from the city of Buzzuluk. I finally was informed that 15 miles farther in a colony "Donskoy" there was a new shoemaker by the name of Adolf Kuhn. "That is him." I set out. That proved to be about 90 miles from Buzzuluk. I had already 75 miles laid behind me and another 15 miles to walk with a well satisfied stomach was a pleasure.

Arriving at Donskoy I found a large beautiful colony where all the buildings were in straight rows on each side of the road. Gigantic trees shaded the streets. I started inquiring for my loved ones and soon was directed to their home. With trembling joy I knocked at the door and in a moment I was in the arms of my sister Olga. At last I found a Haven of Refuge.

I also learned of them that Fredrick was around in these colonies. He, of course, was not absolutely at freedom, as he was there hiding to keep out of army life. He was working for a farmer. I soon located him and thoughts of past experiences were exchanged.

Adolf had made very good financially with his shoemaking ability and was equipping himself for the trip back to the Ukraine. This trip could only be made by horses, as the railroads were as yet all broken up because of the revolution. So Adolf and his brother, Theodore, and many others bought horses and wagons and formed a large caravan of those previous exiled people who had escaped death and were hiding among these dear people in the Mennonite colony.

The war was now over and the revolution was also subdued, so naturally these folks from the Ukraine longed to go back to their old homes. Among this caravan homeward bound, I too, was found.

CHAPTER X

On the Road Back to the Ukraine

A caravan of seven different families, approximately twenty-one wagon loads, formed one group. These were all of such people who were exiled in 1914 and had survived out of the war, Revolution, and famine days. There was a mixture of different ages, some quite old folks, and also little folks, and even infants such as little Water Kuhn, my nephew, who was only about one month old when we left, homeward bound.

At the beginning it appeared to be rather an enjoyable trip. It happened in July, 1920, so the days and nights were warm. We did not make very much progress due to the fact that our horses had to live mainly on grazing. Whenever we found some good pasture we just stayed over for a day or so to give our faithful horses a chance to fill up. On an average it was calculated that we made about fifteen or, at the most, twenty miles per day.

The construction of wagons in Russia during that time was very crude. They had only wooden axles and all wooden wheels even without an iron rim around them. You could have heard us for miles. Those poor old wagons squeaked and groaned very much indeed.

Onward we went, slow but sure. Finally we left even the last Mennonite colony behind us and no sooner were we in the famine stricken areas. It was amazing what a difference there was. It looked to us as if the Lord had shielded His people in the same manner as He shielded the children of Israel in Egypt.

These famine stricken countries were not very pleasant places to go through. In fact, they were extremely dangerous villages to go through, for when people are starving, they are not very kind to their neighbors who still have some food. For this very reason we avoided passing through towns or villages and stuck mainly to the smaller roads and usually camped overnight in some forest or field. One day after climbing a very steep hill where we only could go a few steps and then put rocks under the wheels so as to give our horses their wind, we finally reached the top and were greatly surprised to find good grazing. There we camped for the night. However, during the night time our horses showed great discomfort. They would not go into the bush but only hung around the wagons, and moreover, we could tell they were in fear when they snorted and trembled. In a short time when darkness seized upon us, we found ourselves compassed about with timber wolves howling and coming upon us. We would have been a prey to these beasts had we not have been so great a company. The only way we could protect our horses was by kindling a fire all around the camp and keeping it up all night. Somehow the wolves were afraid of fire.

The next day we started down those chalk mountains and it was not such an easy task. We had to tie the wheels of the wagons and skid down. A serious accident could have happened if it had not been for God's protecting hand upon us. The wagon in which Olga and Walter were riding, broke the rope, and down they came as fast as the horses could gallop. When we saw it we didn't think they would survive. (However, may I add at this time that little Walter at the time of this writing, was a technical Sergeant in the U. S. Army all through the Second World War.) All things are possible with God. By this time we were over a month on our way when we met with poisoned water in a pond. Several of our horses that drank thereof died. One of Adolf's horses fell, too, leaving us with over-loaded wagons. Not very often did we have a chance to ride before, but from now on, everybody had to walk and the horses only pulled our belongings.

During this time of slow progress, we one day were surrounded by bandits or perhaps in a truer sense of the word, compassed about with hungry starving people. Upon discovery that we had much flour with us we were forced to give it up to this famine stricken village. At first our menfolk tried to defend themselves, but soon found out that the only way to get away alive was to give up anything they might ask and they asked plenty. We were stripped of practically all our food supply.

Shortly after this procedure we met up with a horse epidemic, "distemper." This took a great toll on our horses. We then were forced to change our plans to go home all the way by horses. All agreed to stick together and so an agreement was reached that everyone would sell all they had and pool it together, then rent a boxcar on the train to the Ukraine. The trains here were all in running order and we all were indeed very tired of going by team, as we had covered some 700 miles since we left the Mennonite colony in the province of Samara. Now we were in Central Russia in the city of "Kuznetsk." Here in the city Kuznetsk we had the dreadful experience of losing a member of our family, Theodore Kuhn's wife's sister, Agata, a young girl about 17 who was with us. She was a very pretty girl indeed. She went uptown and never returned; neither to this day was it ever learned what became of her. No doubt she was caught by the White Slavery gang, as that was a very common thing in Russia to happen to nice looking girls.

Our caravan on arriving at Kuznetsk had camped near the railway tracks near the city. During this time I was watching the horses as they were feeding alongside the track. It happened that a train ran down a calf about a year old. After seeing the accident I located the owner of the calf. He came out and looked it over. I asked him if we could have the meat. This was granted and so I was able to supply our entire camp with fresh veal.

During these two weeks in Kuznetsk we were all able to sell our heavy belongings and at last boarded a train for the last run from Kuznetsk to Walynsk, which is the capital city of the Province Wolynean in which Adolf's farm home was located.

However, we were only gone to the next large city, Pensa, where we had to go through a censor taking down all our details of our exile, etc. In order words, we were not coming home, but immigrating into the Ukraine from Siberia. There were, literally, hundreds and hundreds of them awaiting the same turn to be permitted immigration. It took about three weeks when at last our name was called. By this time we were financially broke and had to live under the open sky again while snow covered the ground as in the days of exile in 1914.

A dreadful accident occurred which I must mention before closing this chapter. A number of us children were sitting next to the rails playing where two old men having laid a railroad tie across the rails were sawing wood. Suddenly a locomotive gave a bump to the row of cars on the rails where we immigrants were in, and when the car next to the tie crossing the road struck the tie, it jumped off the rails and landed upon us children playing there. One little girl about seven or eight years old was pinned under a wheel. This was a very pathetic sight. The poor little girl had to lie there with her leg pinned under the wheel for almost an hour before we could get the wrecking men there to lift up the car. Of course, her leg had to be amputated.

As I look back upon all the suffering, loss of lives, loss of limbs and health, etc., I just marvel how I escaped over and over again. Not that I was in the least any better or stronger than any of these who died and were crippled and maimed for life – no, perhaps I was the weakest of them all, but I was left alive to tell the story.

All this was brought upon the poor innocent folks because some wicked blood-thirsty children of the devil wanted war. There will be a settlement some day before the Great White Throne of God and I believe we who are born again will have to appear before this judgment as witness against those who rejoiced in our sufferings while on earth. Oh, Lord! Come quickly to judge the nations. This is my cry. "Therefore be ye also ready; for in such an hour as ye think not the Son of Man cometh." (Matthew 24:44).

CHAPTER XI

My Life Amongst Relatives

Can you imagine our joy and thankfulness when at last in the second week of November, 1920, we arrived at the station of "Novograd Wolynsk," the home station of the Kuhns? Although this was not my home, I greatly rejoiced with them in being back again in the Ukraine.

Over six years had passed since we all left our homes in 1914 to be exiles and refugees of war. Let me assure you that it felt good to be back.

Mr. Emil Kuhn, the oldest brother of Adolf, had come to the station with a conveyance to take us to their old home. The station was about 30 miles from their home. Emil had arrived home a year ahead of us and of course everything was somewhat straightened out, so it did not mean to get back to an empty, deserted and broken home, but into a family reunion. As mentioned, the Kuhns lived in the Province of Wolynsk in a little village called "Rudakopf." It was customary in that area to have the house, granary and barn all under one roof. In a way it was very handy for them, as they could do all the chores without even stepping outdoors; but whether it was very sanitary, I have my doubts.

The house was a large one, yet after all the sons came back bringing their new wives with them, it proved too small of them all. I looked around for a job amongst the farmers. Of course, jobs were hard to find in those days when people were just turning back from exile, but the good Lord helping me, I found a job feeding cattle and pasturing them in the summertime. My year around wages were 20 rubles ($10.00) a year and the boss would plant one bushel of potatoes for me and I would be the owner of the crop of potatoes. This was considered very good wages and I was expected to work hard for such good income.

In the wintertime all his grain had to be threshed by the fail on the granary clay floor and fanned by throwing the grain with the shovel into the air so that the wind would blow out the chaff. Then the grain was sacked and stored away in the attic of the house. Next to this I had the job of feeding a large herd of pigs and cattle and milk three cows three times each day.

In the summer it was my job to help the men put the grain into the ground. All the grain had to be sown by hand, and plowed under with a one-shear plow and harrowed with a one-horse harrow. In the harvest time the grain had to be cut with a scythe and bound by hand. After working for this man about two years I really developed muscles. The food was good and work plentiful summer and winter like.

In the meantime, Olga had written to some of our relatives living in the Province of "Kieff" in a town called "Bozar." It was Mrs. Julius Geike, a sister to my mother. Her husband, Mr. Geike, was a miller in a flour mill in this town. This place was about 125 miles away from Rudakopf. One day Olga received a letter asking me to come to them and that uncle would get me a job in the flour mill. As soon as my time with my boss was up I left on my journey for Bozar. From my wages I was able to buy me a suit of clothing, a nice pair of high-top boots as per Russian style, and also a short fur coat made of sheepskin. I started out on my usual way of travel, which was walking every step of the way. The roads were very muddy, so muddy that I could only with great difficulty make any headway at all. But each step brought me nearer, so I just kept going. After having put 30 miles behind me, I came to a village called "Lesowtchisia" where I knew one of my aunts, Mrs. Schmuland, lived. She was also a sister of my mother. I will never forget this trip. The mud was so deep that sometimes my boots almost refused to stay on my feet, but I was determined to get there, and I got there. No one knew me there. My aunt did not recognize me until I told her who I was. When this was done, I experienced kind motherly arms around me, which I had missed so deeply ever since my darling mother had died.

Their family was large, being eight children. I fitted right in the bunch and indeed was treated as one of theirs. For two weeks I visited with them until the roads were fit to go on. I once more set out on my journey to Kieff, having about another 95 miles ahead of me. Starting out on this journey, my uncle took me 20 miles on my way with a team, which was a wonderful lift. Only 75 miles ahead; that was easy: I walked like on springs; sleeping in barns or straw stacks overnight was perfectly okay with me. On my journey I came to a large four mill and here I endeavored to stay overnight. The owner of the mill, after I had made my acquaintance, happened to know my father and even my grandfathers, so I was a welcome guest with them. This was on a Saturday so I stayed with them over Sunday, as I never walked on Sundays, for I wanted to attend church.

Monday morning very early I set out on my last lap of the journey. It was only 30 miles to the town of Bozar. I walked those 30 miles that day, arriving quite late at the place. Inquiring for the home of the miller, I was soon at the right door. No one knew me in this home. After a few questions of different matters, I identified my-self to them as Marzelius Hausmann. Again I felt motherly arms embracing me. Aunt Mathilda was so much like mother that I could not help but weep for joy. Yes, beloved reader, the joy seemed boundless, especially when they took me to the next room and there was Grandma, mother's mother, who so many times before the exile watched over us. Poor old Grandma, she was now 75 years old. When she heard me tell of my experiences and the death of my mother, her loving daughter, Tofielea, it just about broke her heart. She would hug me and love me trying to express all her love for the entire Hausmann family to me. I was the only one she ever saw back from the exile from our family.

God had been wonderful to me. My heart was filled with praise to Him who made it possible for me to see dear old Grandmother. Here I could enjoy again what it meant to have a home. The children, of whom there were seven, were just like my own sisters and brothers and aunt and uncle were just like father and mother to me.

After I had settled down, I wrote to my sisters, Herta and Mathilda and also to Fredrick. I told them to try to get home as I had, among relatives and Grandma, etc. I well recall the day when I said goodbye to them in the cholera stricken city of Orenburg and they had not heard from me since then. Perhaps they thought I had perished somewhere as a boy of twelve years old. Now I was almost 15 years old, was back home, and had conquered the famine and pestilences. Mathilda wrote back that the famine had now been subdued and that they were living much better. In fact, Herta was married. She married a government man in an important office in the city. And Mathilda was engaged to a very fine young man, a banker of a government bank in the city and apparently had no intention to leave now. These men, however, were Communists, but were really kind to the girls as per the report of Mathilda. Of Fredrick, I however, did not hear from until later years.

Herta's name was now Mrs. Mescherokoff and Mathilda's name was to be perhaps in a few years Mrs. Plushonoff. However, at this time of her engagement, she was only 17 years old.

"Lo, I am with you always, even to the end of the world," said Jesus. And He is a wonderful Father to orphans as we who have experienced can affirm. Always when it was darkest before us, God showed us the way out where countless died. He led us through as a fireman would rescue and lead people through the burning to save their lives. All glory be to His precious Name.

I thank God for a praying mother. I think it is the greatest gift God can give to a child on this side of heaven – a godly praying mother. So many, nowadays, do not have praying mothers. I personally consider them extremely unfortunate; in fact, I believe the name "Mother" is too precious to give to a woman that will not pray for her children.

CHAPTER XII

I became Self-Supporting

Of course, ever since I was ten years of age and mother died, I was self- supporting, but what I mean in this chapter is that I became an earner of money and not a beggar as previously explained. My uncle Julius took me with him each day to the mill and taught me very diligently how to operate a machine. The first thing I had to learn was how to stoke it. Wood was used for fuel. It was hard labor to stoke a stream engine. Next was oiling skill, or in other words, the general upkeep of the mechanism.

As soon as I was fairly well acquainted with this type of work I joined the labor union, for otherwise it was impossible to get any job in Russia. Every type of work was controlled by the labor union. I then went through a test in regards to my knowledge as to mechanical work and soon was accepted and received my first job. My first appointment was as fireman in a lovely flour mill only five miles away from Uncle Julius' mill. This indeed was the Lord's wonderful guidance. My uncle, of course, had something to do with it. My wages to begin with were thirteen rubles a month but were raised the next month to 25 rubles. My board and lodging cost me seven rubles per month, so you see I began to save money.

Before I proceed with my own personal experiences, I would like to describe somewhat the custom and manner of living of these people in whose villages I made my home. The village of Nedaschka was fairly large with about 3,000 population. The people were apparently all Ukrainians, with a few Jews holding down the business end of it.

People had built their homes according to their taste, making the streets rather irregular. There wasn't one street that went straight for a long distance. Some would like to have his home so close to the street that the street would have to bend to get around him. The houses were small with doors very low so that you could not walk straightly into the house, but had to bow before you could get into any home. The construction was made out of logs and plastered with clay and cow manure. The inside was only of one room, the floors being of hard clay. One-fourth of the house was taken up with a "peatch," a Russian oven. This oven served for baking, cooking, and also sleeping on top of it. The entire family, men, women and children from grandma to grandchild would sleep on the oven. This, of course, is very nice when it is cold. You do not need any covers; you just toast one side at a time.

Their food is mainly soup, "borsht," and is served in one big bowl and eaten with a wooden ladle (spoon). In fact, it was on the very same principle as we found it in Siberia, Russia. Breakfast was always buckwheat pancakes and bacon and, of course, lots of milk. As for my sleeping accommodations, they never did ask me to sleep with them on the peatch, but made me a bed each night on a large trunk standing in a corner of the house. I was very glad of it, I assure you.

Every Saturday night the whole family, men, women and children go into a steam bath-house; each farmer has his own. Here they steam their bodies until they are red like a beet. Every cold or sickness is steamed out of you. Then after the bath, they come to the house to drink hot tea. Some men who are used to it will drink as much as ten or fifteen glasses. They do not use cups in Russia to drink tea with. You drink your tea in glasses and saucers, with a lump of sugar. The next day after a going over like that, they feel stronger and healthier. I personally could never stand it in those steam baths with them. They would beat their bodies with birch switches made into a broom to the extent that you would think the hide would be cut to the bone. I always preferred going in last or first. In fact, I can only recall twice that I was with them in their wild methods of cleaning themselves. If ever one faints, which is quite frequent, he is taken to the door and cold water is poured over him. As far as I know they never lost one patient in their method of madness, and I do know that many sicknesses were cured by it (if you could take it!).

There is much to be told about this people, but time and space will not permit. I will tell you of another good cure they have - that of eating garlic and onions until every sickness will flee out of their body.

I could tell you of their farming system and their wooden wagons without a nail or any other iron on it. I could tell you of how women folks spin and weave and produce all the clothes from underwear to overcoats out of flax straw and wool. I could tell you about their religion and social life, but all that is not what I have set out to do at this time. So here we go back to my own personal life experiences.

The mill where I worked was not what you call large, but it did have two departments, a flour mill and an oil mill, where we made oil out of flax or linseed and sunflower seeds. My job as stoker was a heavy one, but I did not mind it as my health was good and I had lots to eat.

After about six months I was promoted to the engineering job and another man was put on as my stoker. I then began to rise in the labor union and received my diploma as engineer and my wages were raised to 45 rubles. Now I could afford to board at a better place. The stoker man, Mr. Wisbond, a Jew, proposed to me to board among Jewish people. To this I gladly consented, and through his help, he being a Jew, obtained a fine place with a quite well-to-do Jewish family. Of course I had to get used to the Jewish type of eating. It indeed was entirely different and by far not as rich and nourishing as in the

Ukrainian home. Having learned to be content in whatever state I was, I soon felt quite at home with the Jews. Moreover, I learned their language, "Yiddish," which was very much the same as German. After living with them a year I could have passed as a Jew any place. In fact, I attended their synagogues and pretended to be a Jew. The board at this place cost me 20 rubles but we two boys had our private room and each one his private bed. Our house lady also did our laundry for the same price.

In this manner I worked at this mill in Nedaschka for over two years. I enjoyed my work and saved up some money. My intentions at the time were to go back to our old home in Minsk and again build the old Hausmann residence. In the year 1925, the mill where I worked burned down for some unknown reason and I was left without a job for a while. I went back to my uncle's place and there decided to go to my old home where the cradle once stood.

CHAPTER XIII

Back Where the Cradle Stood

Before I tell you about my experiences on the journey home and about my old home, I would like to acquaint my reader with three members of our family. If you look back in the first chapter, "The Introduction," you will find stated that my father had three daughters by his former marriage. When I was a child they were grown up. In fact, two were married while one was working in a sugar factory in the city of Minsk. So it was natural for me not to know them. When I returned back home to our old farm, I found them there, and, of course, made good acquaintance with them, particularly Martha, the oldest. I also saw and learned to know Emilia and Lidya. All three of them at this time were married and living in the vicinity of our old home.

Our home in Minsk was about 70 miles from the little city Bozar where my uncle lived. I made a list of all the villages I had to pass on my way home. Seventy miles in that country is a long distance, when every step of the way has to be covered on foot. In my case, having had some money, I hired a farmer to take me the first 45 miles to where a relative of ours lived. From there I endeavored to walk. After a day's visit I started out on my walking journey. I was used to walking, and 25 to 30 miles was nothing to me. I could easily walk that in one day. On my way I came into one place that used to be a Jewish village. There I saw many empty houses. Going into one of them, I saw some gruesome things. The walls were all scratched as by fingernails. They were blotched with blood which was old and faded by now. I went to a farmer asking him what all those empty houses meant. He told me that was where they had massacred the Jews. He told me that hundreds of them were put to death there in the most unimaginable cruelty, that of slowly cutting them to death while they ran around in the house in madness of pain. When I heard this I made haste to get out of this village. It brought back afresh to me the days of the revolution. This massacre against the Jews was done by the party "Machnowtzy" who declared themselves as enemies of the Jews.

Not far from this village I had to go through a mighty forest of fir and spruce trees. It is not always safe in Russia to go through a forest alone. Somehow, I was not familiar with fear so I went in and practically all that day was found in this forest. I saw there high towers built, towering way above the tall fir trees. I walked over to one of them, looked at it, saw carvings in the timbers, and to my great amazement, found my father's name carved into those beams with other names. I then recalled that my father used to build these towers in this forest. What a wonderful thing it seemed to me to make this discovery. It was to me as if I stood on holy ground to be where dear dad had worked years gone by. I just threw my arms around those old timbers and wept bitterly.

I had not walked so very far when I saw another one of this same type. I walked up to it, too, and found the same incarvement. It looked quite sturdy, so I climbed up and had a wonderful view over the treetops. What a blessed memory came back to me when in childhood father would come home from work and we children would run to meet him and love him and be loved of him. Now it was just a memory that had faded far into the past.

At sunset I arrived in a colony "Klotchin." Here lived one of my uncles, mother's brother. I found their place. They had not heard of any of us since we were exiled in 1914 and were amazed to see me. They thought that the entire Hausmann family had died out. I visited with them for two days and then set forth on my journey which was but another ten or fifteen miles.

I came near what was once known as our home, in the little village "Katkie." Walking through it, I saw that little hill with spruce trees all over it. Here I hoped to find my old home sweet home. But oh, how changed it looked to me. Those tiny little spruce trees were all large tall trees and to my amazement, I failed to see that lovely new house father had built a year before our exile. For a while I wondered if it was the right place after all. I saw people living in what I thought was our barn. Walking up to it, I was met by a woman with a couple of small children. I asked her, "Is this Katkie?" "Yes." She answered. "Is this Frank Hausmann's place?" "Yes." "Are you Mrs. Roloff?" Again I heard the affirmative answer. Again I took a look around. Could this be our home, the home I so longed to see for those many years gone by? The woman was still looking at me, perhaps wondering who I was. I then said, "Martha, I am Marzelius, your brother." She wept for joy as she put her arms around me to welcome me home.

Such was my homecoming. Instead of the whole family returning from the exile, it was only I, one of a family of 12 that ever again saw the old dear place. What a change there was. The lovely new house was taken away and only the cellar hole was to be found. The old barn had been fixed up and converted into a house by Mr. Roloff, Martha's husband.

The next day I walked over the entire farm looking over the land, etc. I found the little stream "Ritchka" where we youngsters used to love to swim. It was a blessed memory and that is all. I knelt down and asked the Lord to lead me. I asked Him to answer the prayer of my dear mother for my life. Oh, how I wished that all the past would have been a dream and I could have been gathered into mother's arms as eleven years ago before the exile.

I went back to the so-called home of my sister and told her of my heart-breaking discoveries. My heart was as heavy as lead. I told them that they could have the farm if they liked. I didn't want anything from it even though I was rightly the heir to it. I there and then freed myself from my heirship as to the Hausmann estate. Albert, Martha's husband, showed me with what poverty he had to contend. He had no horse because he, too, had only returned a year ago, so he farmed the land with a spade and harrowed it with a little harrow, he himself being the horse to draw it. The farm was not very large, only 24 acres, but it was too large for one man to work with a spade. I bade them goodbye with God's blessing. My property was from henceforth theirs.

I then went to see my other two sisters, Emilia and Lidya. After visiting them for a day at each place, I went to see one more of my uncles, mother's brother Gustaf Ebert, and then I was on my way back to Bozar. At every one of these places that I visited I was greeted as a person who was given up for dead. I stopped off at many of our friends and relatives and could not leave until I had told them all about our experiences since 1914. I hired a farmer to take me back. One of my cousins, Bertha Ebert, Uncle Gustaf's daughter, accompanied me to Bozar to visit with Uncle Geikes. I indeed enjoyed this trip much more than walking, though it was only on a farmer's wagon without springs, but the company and the rest did me much good. The visit to my old home was an experience to me that will never be forgotten as long as I live.

I was indeed glad to see the old home place. Even though it was in ruin, it blessed my heart to see it and to weep where my loved ones had wept. Yes, I recalled that lovely vegetable garden where mother and I had gone before we were taken into exile. I vividly saw in my memory how she broke down in tears when she had to leave it all and flee. I recalled how I supported her there until she fainted that tragic day of our departure. I could find some pieces of old toys that I played with as a little child. All seemed precious, all seemed sacred to me, but I could not stay very long, for my tears were streaming from me without control.

CHAPTER XIV

Back to Work

The first thing I did after returning from my holiday trip was to report to the worker's union. They in turn were glad to see me back, as a job was awaiting me there of relieving the engineer at Bozar, where my uncle worked as a miller. I very much appreciated this. However, it was only for one month while the engineer had his holidays.

During this time in 1924, the government tried to do away with money and run Russia on the trading system. This proved to be another one of Mr. Lenin's five-year failures. For instance, my wages were 50 bushels of rye flour per month. One-third went for my board and 33 bushels were left over. I couldn't fine storage room for it, and neither could I buy anything for it as grain that year was plentiful. No one cared to accept it for products such as clothing, etc. It proved to be an extremely unreasonable method. For instance, if a farmer wanted to buy some little things such as soap and needles, etc., he had to take a cow or horse or calf to trade it for the products he chose to buy. The government, of course, saw that it was most ridiculous and new money was again printed known as the new "Cherwontzy" Reds.

During this year, which was Lenin's last year on earth, Mr. Lenin did a lot of experimenting. It was this year that he tried the union farming system as the five-year plan of collective farming. The first thing they did was to pool the farms together and make a government farm out of it. All were to work together and all were to eat together as one family. The first thing we noticed was the fact that ambition of the working man was killed. You were to work eight hours per day. Then we noticed that as soon as the time was up, everybody dropped his tools or implements and went home to fight with his wife or fellowman.

Among the women folk we noticed that there wasn't that loving spirit which the government thought to promote. If you put 25 or 30 women into one kitchen, you will agree that it will be a rowdy, loud kitchen, especially when each woman knows how to cook the soup the best.

The next thing we noticed was among the children. You put about 200 or more youngsters together, as they were in these union farms, all living under one roof, and all eating at one table, and all playing in one yard, and you will understand how they will get into fights. Of course, each child will run to its own mother to complain and each mother will naturally defend her own child. So the women folks would get into fights over the children. This is the sight you would see. They would head for the door and grab one another by the hair. You would see hair flying every direction and screaming to high heaven. You have no idea how women folks can scream until you see a real fight among them. When the men folks would see the women folks fighting, they would come to defend their own wives, which is very nice and the proper thing to do. (I hope you defend your own wife and not your neighbor's wife.) You could see them clubbing one another down mercilessly; filling the hospital with wounded and killed ones. This was a daily procedure in this union government farm.

The government saw that this would not do; it was the children they said that caused all the trouble. They then built what was known as an institution to raise children. But the mothers would not stand for it. Each mother wanted her own little one for herself. They took them away at the day of their birth and placed them in these institutions to be raised by the government nurses. The mothers, however, armed themselves to fight to deliver their own children. The government had a regular revolution going on with the women folks.

Another step was taken to kill motherly love and that

was known as the free love system. They took the females from one farm and interchanged them with the other. No more was family life respected; they were to live as cattle. This, however, brought a ruin to the nation. In less than a year, the majority of them were shamefully diseased to such an extent that in order to save the race, the physicians who had declared them incurable, demanded to do away with them. Numbers literally counting into hundreds, and mostly young people, were called out and taken out of the camp and mowed down with the machine gun. Such was the five-year plan of Mr. Lenin's union farming.

I worked during that time with my Uncle Julius in the city of Bozar. During that time, my uncle taught me the job of being a miller, as that was a higher paid position and also a clearer job. When my term was up, which lasted for about three months instead of just one month as I had previously been advised, I was a full-fledged miller and was appointed by the union for a job of this nature. There was a new mill erected about 45 miles from Bozar which was to be my place. I worked there for about a year with fairly good success, drew good wages, and had a nice living place with two elderly Christian people by the name of Potzwold. Then the union appointed me to a job in the woods. There was a mill there which was also a sawmill. They sawed lumber during the daytime and I ground flour at night. This was a very lonely place as no one lived there except the workers. No one cared to take this place, so they put me there because I was a young single man about 17 years of age at this time. It was in 1925. The people there were of the lower class. All the workers were heavy drunkards. I was introduced to drinking and many times forced to drink. I could not find a place where I could read my New Testament which I always had with me. It was here where I lost out with my Lord. I became a drunkard deep in sin.

One day in a half drunken state, I went down to the

transmission where these powerful gears roll in terrific speed. I wanted to end my life, for my sins were haunting me day and night. I closed my eyes and was just about to cast myself into those revolving gears, but at that moment it was to me as if I heard my mother say, "I am praying for you, my son." In amazement and astonishment I looked around, for the voice seemed distinct. I fell on my knees and asked God for forgiveness. Oh, I thank God for having had a praying mother. If it had not been for those prayers, I would have been in hell all these many years, in a Christless drunkard's grave.

Shortly after this, in God's great infinite mercy, He caused this whole sinful hell hole to be burned up, and I was glad of it. I went back to Bozar to my uncle's place. This was home to me in the presence of Aunty Mathilda, who was so much like mother that I respected her like my own mother. Grandma's presence, too, made it double home to me. I have no picture of my mother, but when you look at Aunty Mathilda, you can see in her my mother.

Having lived at home for a few days, I saw the wonderful hand of God in it all. Yes, Romans 8:28 is still in the Book. With but one blast of fire I was delivered out of the jaws of hell. After living with my folks for a while, I straightened up again and cleaned up my life, and I knew also that God had forgiven me. However, there were scars of sin left in my body that I had to contend with. The carving of liquor was with me for years. Smoking also had taken control of my infirmities.

My uncle told me that the union was appointing him to a new job in a brand new mill about 20 miles from Bozar, in a little village "Wercholeska." This mill was to be operated by diesel power and he suggested that I make my application for it. To this I gladly agreed and sure enough, I got the job. Never before had I operated a diesel, but my heart was in it and there was no one to compete with me in this job, as there was no engineer in this particular union capable for a diesel power machine. I enjoyed my work. It was new, but interesting, and I lived together with my folks. The mill was located near a very lovely little lake and our house, a new construction, was built close to it.

During that time, the Communistic party was very interested in getting all the union workers to become Communists. Uncle and I didn't have much use for them, but in order to be at peace with them, we, too, were signed up to their views and attended their conferences and also schools of education. The requirements of a Communist were - first, you had to be 21 years of age. You had to see eye to eye with their setup and be convinced in your heart that there is no other government on earth that can come equal to it. You have to swear in the name of the power of communism that you will deny, destroy, and bring to naught any powers of government opposing the communistic viewpoint. Also you must be willing to live and to die for communism. After the required agreement has been reached, you graduate from the "Komsomol" to Communists. With the graduation you received authority and with this authority you receive your graduation present, which is a revolver. With this weapon you can shoot anybody, either man or women, if they oppose you or your communistic viewpoints. A Communist in other words is a chosen, elect person who has the right over the life of the common people.

Let me assure you, my dear reader, that a country with this kind of a law where boys of 21 years old, and some no more mature than a 16 year old youngster, are able to walk around with such a weapon and so great liberty and authority is a dangerous country to live in.

One month out of each 12 we were entitled to a vacation. In my case, I had to go three months overtime because during this year I carelessly had two points of my front fingers cut off by the machine and had to spend one month in the hospital and another two months at home before I could go back to my job again. However, when the required month was up, I took my vacation and took a little trip to see my sister Olga at Rudokoph where I left five years ago,

CHAPTER XV

On My Holidays

Five years since I left the Kuhn's have slipped by. I well recall the day when I started out on foot to make this journey to my uncle's place in Bozar to seek adventures of life. At this time, in less than five years, I needed not come back walking, but I could take the train. The Lord had been with me, prospering my journey. But was I as faithful to Him as He was to me? Rather shamefully, I must confess that I was not.

Arriving at my nearest station in "Malin" I took the train which in one day brought me to "Novagrad Wolynsky," the station nearest Rudokopf. From here I was able to take the bus, as in those days Russia had commenced the bus line between larger cities. This was the first car or bus ride I had ever had in my life. Arriving at my sister's home, I was greatly surprised when they looked at me rather suspiciously, for I came there in a Communist uniform and was saturated with nicotine from smoking. I indeed was well-dressed, but that did not fool my sister. She knew that I had lost out with the Lord. After a lovely dinner with them, I pulled out a package of cigarettes but did not care to smoke them as Olga right there gave me a good lecture reminding me of mother's prayers and the fact that mother had dedicated me to preach the Gospel of the Lord Jesus Christ. I tried to be decent and tried to put on a good front that I was still a Christian boy, etc. but my visit with them became uneasy to me, as well as to them, as they could see I was of a different nature. Pretense of Christianity is very obnoxious to people who know the Lord as their personal Saviour and friend. However, they did not ignore me, but invited me with them to their Christian endeavors.

At the same time, I learned that they were preparing to

go to America. In fact, they had practically all their needed documents. Hearing this, it stirred up in me a desire to go to America. Ever since in 1913 when I was five years of age when one of my uncles, "Fredrick Ebert," left for America, there was planted in my heart a desire for America. On his farewell, he came to us and took Mathilda, my sister, and me in his arms and said, "When you grow up, you come to America. I'll be seeing you there." I never forgot that. All through my days of suffering, every once in a while it came to me, "When you grow up, you come to America." At this time there seemed to rise a star for me to guide me in this long desired journey and new world. But how can this be brought about? Immigration was only granted to Canada and that only to farmers; whereas, I was an engineer by trade, a Communist to be, and also of military age, 18 years old. At the time it looked absolutely hopeless. I took the train to Kijew to have an interview with the immigration authorities; but I was absolutely discouraged and, in fact, threatened that if I, a prospective Communist, would leave Russia during my military age, I would be facing the firing squad without mercy.

This sounded to me rather hopeless but not all together convinced to dismiss the thought. I took the next train back to Rudokopf and made known this hopeless situation. My brother-in-law, Adolf, was a man who always seemed to find an answer to problems of this nature. He and I went to a well-known friend of his, a Jew, who was then in business to help immigration. After telling him my case, he told me that it would cost me about 50 rubles to straighten this matter out. Gladly I laid down this amount. Now in order to make this story as short as possible, I shall not try to tell you how this clever Jew went about it, but in a few short days I was two years younger and I was a farmer in good standing which, of course, entitled me to an immigration visa should I so desire.

The next thing demanded of me was a Confirmation to which the Jewish lawyer could not help me. I went to an elderly Lutheran Pastor in the city of "Schitomir" and he gave me the Catechism to memorize. This I did. I went to my hotel room and started in. The next day I went back to him and he took me to his beautiful church and confirmed me. Presenting this new document to my good lawyer, the Jew, he encouraged me that this was all I needed now to apply for my immigration visa. Of course, you must understand this was done at a different council than I interviewed first in Kijew. In fact, it was done in a different state of Russia.

In about one month, my needed documents arrived and to my great surprise, I was booked to go at the same time and the same boat as the Kuhns were booked. This indeed gave me great joy in spite of the fact that I was not at all worthy of all this wonderful grace of God. I was freed as a bird from a cage to flee from Russia.

I took the train for Malin and got home to my uncle's place, spreading the news that I would at once leave for America, yet I had to keep it silent from the labor union and the Communist parties. It was best for me to slip away as quickly and quietly as possible. Indeed I found it hard to leave aunty and uncle and all those fine cousins of mine who were to me just like my own brothers and sisters. They had eight children; the oldest was 13 and the youngest one year old. The hardest of all was to say goodbye to old Grandma. She was now 81 years old and I knew I would never see her alive on this earth again. As I stood in regard to my spiritual condition, I had really no hopes of ever seeing her up yonder. She knew it and her last challenge to me was to meet her in Heaven. Oh, how I thank God as Timothy of old, I had a praying grandmother and a praying mother. (II Timothy 1:5) A young man may shake off a good sermon being preached or he may forget his pastor's prayer, but he cannot so easily shake off or forget the prayer of mother or grandmother.

In the month of March, 1927, I left the old blood-soaked Russian soil behind me, Glory! Glory! What a joy! A new world, a new life, a new people, with a new language ahead of me.

Rev. Mark Houseman and His Family, taken in 1954. Phil. 1:21.

The Author's three Sisters: Olga, Adina, and Herta, taken 1918, when they worked in a restaurant in the city of Orenburg, just before Adina died.

My Aunt Mathilda, Mrs. Julius Geike, and their family.

A Railroad Station, with refugees to be shipped to Siberia.

Inside the Railroad Station, a common every-day scene.

Slave Labor, the hard work is always done by women.

My Brother Frederick, to the right, as missionary among the Tartar Mohammedans, after he fled from the Soviet persecution of Christians.

My Sister Herta, her husband and child, with Mathilda standing in the back. Taken 1935.
Mathilda, that precious little girl who went through that night of suffering when Mother died. She developed into a beautiful young bride at the age of 17, my favorite little sister.

A typical home in the Ukrain Russia with happy women folk visiting.

Common Ukranian men in their best apparel.

When I was 17 years old and signed up to become a Communist at 21 years of age. Note Communist uniform.

Greek Catholic Churches. The globes are overlaid with gold. Located in the city of Kijew alone are probably several hundred of them.

Lenin's Tomb on the Red Square at Moscow.
Sometimes people in rows a mile long waiting to march in, as de- described in chapter 1, part 2.

In every city and many villages throughout Russia you see this monument of Lenin, the man who was the hero of the Revolution in 1917.

Kremlin, the seat of government in Moscow.

In bed for 16½ months; one year flat on my back.

Brother Frederick and his family when he was minister in Buzzuluk.

My Sister Mathilda and her husband, a Russian Jew, a banker, in the city of Orenburg.

From left to right: Mark Houseman, Eric McMurry, Joe Jesperen, and Rob Summerville.

Most of these Baptist ministers suffered death in Siberian exile for the name of Christ.

Quarette No. 2 in 1940: Clare McElheren, Charles Harnstra, Norman Jamisen, and Mark Houseman.

Gospel Quartet No. 3: Joe Dyck at the front; rear left to right: Dave Hart, Vic Long and Mark Houseman.

This happened on March 10, 1943.

Rev. and Mrs. Mark Houseman, when pastor at Fosston, Sask. Canada, and Children: Margaret Isabel, Walter Mark and Josephine

PART II

CHAPTER I

Looking For the New World

It was on the 14th day of March, 1927, when we, a little band from Rudokoph, started out bound for America. This particular company was composed of Adolf, Olga, three of their children, Walter then being five years old, Erick 3, and Erwin only about 6 months, also Theodore Kuhn, his wife and her sister, Olga Kuhn, Adolf's sister and myself. Another young man was also with us who was in the same fear as I was, that if the government finds out of our departure before we crossed the border we both may yet face the firing squad.

Very early that morning we set out to make the first 30 miles by team to our nearest railroad station. Arriving there, we found as we usually found all over Russia, the railroad station jam-packed full of people. The trains coming to the station were loaded inside and outside, people hanging by their hands on it and covering the roofs of the cars like flies. Russia could use about five times as many trains as they have.

When we had our train pointed out to us, we just jammed in with the rest of them. There are no seating capacities in the passenger trains in Russia. There is a three-deck bunk in the center of each car on which all the people pile on, both to sleep and to sit. Most of them were standing, leaning against the walls. I felt extremely sorry for my poor sister Olga. Their little boy cried all day and practically all night long. All the night and part of the next day brought us to Kijew.

You can see this beautiful city for many miles because of the innumerable churches. It has always been the custom with the Greek Catholic church that the peaks of the churches are overlaid with gold, and when the sun shines on it, you just stand in amazement to behold. It looks like many suns sparkling in the air.

Here we had to change to a train bound for Moscow. Again we had to contend with the jammed trains. The way little children roam around the railroad stations in Russia is indescrabable. It indeed reminded me of the time when I, as a little boy in the city of Orenburg, jammed into the railroad stations to keep warm overnight. You would think that by now after the country had ten years of peace, it would have been different, but apparently not so. Russia remains Russia. People multiply so fast that all the wars and pestilences in the world could not keep them down.

This was a most interesting trip from Kijew to Moscow, as this is Russia's most popular division. For one day and two nights we were jammed into this train. Arriving in this wonderful city of Moscow, we were directed to the immigration house. Talk about people; every place was jam-packed full of them. We had no idea there were so many people emigrating out of Russia. Each one had to be personally interviewed by the emigration authorities. This, of course, took time, and so for nine days we were held up in Moscow in this emigration house. We young folks, of course, were up and around each day to see this large three million populated city with its one thousand Greek Catholic churches and probably at least another thousand of other denominations. At that time, the churches were still operating. There was one particular church known as the "Red Square" and this was by far the most visited. It was, in other words, Lenin's tomb, the present god of the Soviet Union. As you well know, in 1923 Lenin died and was embalmed and laid in a glass coffin and placed in the center of the city of Moscow in a tomb that was glistening with gold. The Red Square tomb is a beautiful sight to behold. Around it is a steel fence with armed guards around it. You would see people standing in line, sometimes about a fourth of a mile long. These would be slowly marching into the tomb. I, too, stepped in line to see what I could see. When I reached the Iron Gate, I saw there two policemen checking you over to see if you had any explosives on you. Then you are permitted to enter. When you get to the mouth of the tomb, you are looked over by two policemen who had an awful stern look, so much so, that if you would have dynamite on you, it would explode right there from the very look they give you. On each end of the coffin stands a guard so silently as though made of wax. If it were not for the sweat drops rolling down their faces, you would think they were just artificial men. You must bow lowly, salute the coffin, and go out the next exit. This goes on day after day, year after year, by now for 25 years and still just as strong as ever before. If that is not worship, then pray tell me what is it? God is taken out of Russia to be worshipped, and the embalmed body of Lenin is installed.

When finally our time of departure had come, we were happy people. By this time we all had seen all we cared to see of Moscow. I may say here that Moscow is one of the most beautiful cities I ever saw. I don't think there is a much more active city to be found. The traffic in it was just too much for me even though I was used to city jams, but this was jammed together.

It was on March 26, 1927, that we boarded our last train in Russia. Arriving at the border, all our things had to be searched, every suitcase and trunk had to be inspected and gone over by the customs officers. After this, we again had to go back to our Russian trains and we were taken into Latvia where we had to change trains from the Soviet Union to the Latvian train. Oh, what a difference this was. The trains had seats and they were upholstered. I never saw anything like it in all my life before. Those seats were convertible into beds. We thought we were in heaven. Oh, Russia, dark, backward Russia! The young man that went with us and I, who were always afraid we may yet be facing the firing squad were shaking hands congratulating one another and praising God for the escape out of the clutches of Communism. We were across the border, and that meant we were free, shouting for joy. Praise the Lord for His great, mercy! We had been freed and felt like the slaves must have felt when they were freed from slavery by Abraham Lincoln.

Our next city was Riga. The first thing that met us there was glorious, beyond all expectations, for all the people that stepped off the train received a New Testament or a Bible. Dr. Fettler stood there with a group of young people at the train to give out the Word of God to the Russian refugees. The Word of God was denied them in Russia so what a great joy it was to these dear people to once again hold the Word of God in their hands. We were taken to the immigration house by a beautiful bus. Arriving there we were ushered into a large dining hall where a lovely meal was awaiting us. Then we were appointed to a clean-up house where each one of us had to take a shower bath. All our clothing had to be disinfected and all our belongings likewise. All of us had to appear before the physicians. We were then appointed to a room, each family by itself or each single person by himself. What a change, what decentness. Everybody was treated like a human being, whereas all the years in Russia, I had not seen any difference between cattle and human treatment.

We all felt like new-born babies just washed clean. All the lice we had gathered in our clothing on the filthy jammed trains in Russia were killed when they disinfected our clothing while we were taking a bath. They gave us something to put on our heads to kill all the lice in our hair. No filth was tolerated in this new country.

An announcement was made that special gospel services were being held twice every day for the new immigrants. These services were conducted by the well-known Dr. Fettler, one of America's outstanding men of God.

Many found Jesus as Lord and Saviour under his splendid ministry. I never forgot the lovely New Testament that was presented to me the first day out of Russia by Dr. Fettler's group.

We were held up a little at Riga because one of Adolf's children, Erick, took sick, so Olga and the children had to go to the hospital. We really did not mind to wait. All our board and lodging was well taken care of. All we had to do was to enjoy it. So for 14 days we lived at Riga and really enjoyed it in full. I was out every day sight-seeing. This really was a wonderful life. We had paid our fare, board, lodging, and interpreters all the way to Winnipeg, and it was up to the Pacific Railroad and Liner Company to see that we got there well taken care of and fed.

We also saw that in our Soviet Union clothing we did not fit in with the rest of the people. I had some money on hand, having at least $100.00 over after I paid my fare. So I, as well as the rest of them, bought us new clothing, suits, etc. For the first time in my life I bought a hat. Now we could walk around in the city without the people stopping and looking at us as if to say "you belong to Russia." We also bought new suitcases, as in Russia we were only able to buy baskets made out of willow switches. Now we bought real fine leather or wooden constructed trunks and cases.

The fourteen days were not at all too long for us to wait. As soon as baby Erick was well again, we were appointed to board the ship for London, England. Hallelujah! Praise the Lord! The farther away from Russia, the better we felt.

"The LORD is my rock, and my fortress, and my deliverer; my God, my strength, in whom I will trust." (Psalms 18:2).

CHAPTER II

At Sea

It was on April 7th, 1927, that we boarded the beautiful little boat known as "Baltanik." With great joy in our hearts, we took possession of our assigned berth in this boat. However, looking into the distance upon the sea, there was also a feeling of fear to be found in our hearts. Not being acquainted at sea, we, of course, would imagine a rough sea. Nevertheless, the beauty of nature around us made us soon forget all about what might happen. The sea was most calm and presented itself like a spotless mirror where you could see the sunbeams playing on it. This beauty, however, was superseded at nighttime when the stars and moon began to sparkle in the calm, crystal Baltic Sea. I stood for a long time on the deck admiring the beauty of God's nature. Likewise was the rest at night. It was outstanding. There was just enough of a move to rock you to sleep as if a loving motherly hand was placed on the cradle. No wonder men who have been much at sea never care again to go back on the land.

When morning was come, we could hear from many who had preceded us to the deck, "Land! Land! We are nearing land!" So it was, the lovely calm sea was left behind. Our little boat entered into a canal known as the "Wilhalms Canal." Thus for one whole day, we were on this canal. This was, so far in my life, the most beautiful trip I had ever made. The canal was narrow, and you could not see a great margin of water on either side. This made it appear as if the world was passing on each side of you in a swift move with its most beautiful architect, orchards and flower beds, and everything conceivable that might strike the eye of tourists. Here it was as if it stood still and just let the world of this nature pass by. This was the canal that goes through Germany joining the Baltic Sea with the North Sea. The North Sea is the one that leads to London, England.

Towards evening we entered into the North Sea. Before we could make this entry there was a place known as a lock in the German, "Kiel." The boat had to wait there for about 45 or 50 minutes, as the waters were too shallow for the boat to pass through. When we came into this lock the shores were higher than our boat, but after its appointed time was up, the boat apparently stood higher than the shores. Let me apply this to our life. Many times it seems if everything goes so fine. The world passes by us in its beauty. But lo, there is a shallow place in life and our little bark adrift cannot go through. Then the good Lord leads us into a lock where we patiently have to wait, perhaps in beds of sickness, perhaps in sorrow. While we wait, the waters of life begin to rise and lift us up. As our little boat shot out on its way again as soon as the gates were opened, so do we launch out once more on our life's journey, having been patiently waiting on the Lord and having taken a refill of fuel in the reading of His precious Word and prayer. We then, too, can face the stormy North Sea of life as we that night faced with our little Baltanik boat the stormy North Sea leading to London, England.

The North Sea, as you may know, holds the reputation of being very boisterous. The water is yellow and dirty looking. We were not very far on it when we felt restlessness. We discovered that over our beds were rings hanging. For these we had no use before, but now we soon laid hold of them to keep ourselves from falling out of our bunks. In but a little while we noticed that even our stomachs began to rebel against the food, being churned back and forth in our bodies. The orderlies came around with a bucket for each passenger, telling us that if we felt sick to use them.

Let me assure you that most of us made good use of them too and all around it sometimes.

Our little party composed of Christians gathered into one cabin where we passed practically all night in prayer, and singing of hymns if we were not too seasick.

I was amazed to see what these boats can take. It seemed to us we were bouncing in the water all night like a rubber ball. During the next day it was not quite as bad, although rough enough to suit each one of us. The dining hall during mealtime was mostly empty. No one cared to take any food as long as we were on the North Sea. Oh, how good it felt to see land once more. It was with great joy the next night after having been one night, one day, and part of the next night on the North Sea, to land in London, England. This was now the morning of April 11th, when we first laid our eyes upon the gigantic city of the world in those days.

At the harbor there were many buses awaiting us. All the immigrants were loaded on these and were taken through the city, then loaded on a train and bound for Southampton. Arriving at Southampton, we had to go through another clean-up process and disinfection of all our clothing in the same manner we were put through at Riga, Latvia, just to make sure that all the filth of the Soviet Union was washed off. We also had to once again present ourselves to a physical examination.

In Southampton we were held up for 12 days due to the shortage of boats crossing the Atlantic. We, of course, enjoyed our stay in England, and made the best of those lovely opportunities to see all that we could see. That is all we could do, too, as neither of us could speak the English language. In fact, the English language sounded to me very ridiculous, just as if a flock of geese were chattering.

On April 23rd, we were loaded on a train for Liverpool where after two days we boarded the ship "S. S. Minnedosa," a 15,000 ton liner. This was one of the smaller boats crossing the Atlantic, but we found it comfortable and also quite fast. It made the journey in eight days. This trip was indeed a very interesting experience. During those eight days we had both good and bad weather. There were some days when the dining hall was empty. No one cared to eat, as is often the case when you are on the sea. Only for one day did we meet with dense fog where it seemed to us that the boat did not travel at all, or perhaps, very slowly. Practically every minute they were blowing the whistle. This does become extremely tiring when you have to listen to it for 24 hours.

When you are on a boat for eight days, you do appreciate seeing land again. That was what every one of those 500 passengers was busy doing. On the morning of May 3rd we had the great joy of putting our feet on Canadian soil in the harbor of Quebec. What a joy to know that at last I had reached America. We all felt like a bird released from a cage. Russia had no more claims on us. We were in a free country, and to us, a new world.

CHAPTER III

In Canada

My dream from the age of five years old has been at last fulfilled. You will recall that I mentioned in the previous chapters that in 1913 one of my uncles left Russia for America, and at his departure he told me that if I grew up I should come to America. Ever since that time this was my dream and here I lived to see it fulfilled. Praise the Lord!

At Quebec we were still under the care of the C.P.R. Our tickets were purchased in Moscow all the way to Winnipeg, Canada. So without any delay, we were transferred to Winnipeg. At Winnipeg we were detained for a few days because of the tremendous multitude of immigrants coming in who had to be placed. However, during those days of waiting, we were taken care of free of charge by the Canadian government.

Finally, when our turn came, we were asked where we wanted to go. I, personally, not knowing a thing in the new world, not even understanding a word of English, told them through interpreters to send me wherever I could get a job. Some farmers from Saskatchewan, being in need of farm labor, had sent in requests to send some immigrants to them. This was a little town called "Lockwood." So to Lockwood I went. My brother-in-law happened to have an address of some people who had gone there before, so they too, boarded the train for Lockwood. Arriving there, we had a wonderful experience, both on our way and when there. On this large journey we, of course, saw both good and poor looking country, also large cities and little towns. In fact, we all liked the looks of Winnipeg and also the immediate surroundings, as you could find a little bush here and there. As we came farther west we came to what is known as the Canadian prairies, and did they ever look bare! Likewise, the city of Regina looked rather flat and bare to us. When we finally reached Lockwood, about 100 miles north of Regina, we were amazed at its size as it was a town of 150 population, only one street that you could walk through with a couple of hundred steps. There were two stores, one hardware store, two lumber companies, two large implement shops, and a post office. The business end of it was thriving. The stores were full of people. We also learned that some farmers had as much as three sections of land. It was unknown and unheard of to us that any one man could own so much land; whereas, in Russia, if a farmer had twelve acres of land he thought himself quite well off.

When the farmers heard that immigrants were now coming to the station, they met the train, as labor was very scarce in those days. I was picked out by a fine looking strong farmer and ushered to his car. He saw to it that I got all my baggage and off we were to work.

Arriving at his house, he took me into his home and introduced me to his wife and eight children. All I could answer in English was to smile at them, for that was all I knew of the English language. We had a fine dinner; I enjoyed it greatly. As they were talking to me, I kept smiling back at them. The children soon started laughing. I could do that in English too, so I laughed when they laughed all in pure English, and we had a wonderful time.

After dinner he pointed out to me a bunkhouse that was to be my home. I thought that was fine. He took me to his barn and what a string of horses, 28 of them in the barn. All the horses a farmer has in Russia is one or perhaps two. I could not get it. He hitched six of them up to a disk. I just watched him. He told me to sit on the disk and he delivered to me five lines and one special line for a Broncho. I never had so many lines in my hand in all my life. I just didn't know what to do. He told me to go ahead. I spoke to the horses in Russian. Nah! Nah! But they could not understand Russian, so my boss said to them "get up boys" and away we went. He had given me a piece of paper outlining to me how I was to disk, driving around and around on his land. So I did, but the time came for me to stop. I again spoke to the horses in Russian "Perrr, Perrr," but when they heard that noise, they pricked up their ears and went faster than ever. The only way for me to stop them was to choke them on the lines. What an experience for those poor horses to break in a green foreigner! After I got on to the horse language, I soon got on to the other, too. I began to understand and speak a little English. After I got the drift of the thing, it was not so hard to learn to speak, but please do not ask me to spell, even now, after being over twenty years in America. I still think the English spelling is one of the most ridiculous things ever invented.

All that spring from May 11th when I arrived at Lockwood, to July, I worked for this farmer, never having a chance to hear another language than English. When the seeding time was over, which was two months; I could speak enough English to carry on a conversation. I then went to work on road construction until harvest. This gave me a great opportunity to learn things I never could have learned on the farm. At harvest time I went out with the harvesters and the threshing crew. The wages were $4.00 a day. Soon I was able to pay my debt that I had made on the trip which was $100. When I came to Lockwood I had only 50 cents to my name and a $100 debt, but after the summer was over, I had $400 in the bank.

However, during the winter there was nothing to do around Lockwood. I got together with my brother-in-law and we rented a section of prairie haying land. This we cut the next haying time and so made a job for ourselves by next winter. We each had purchased a team of horses and the haying implements. During the summer we only spent one month or three weeks at it, but during winter time we would press it into bales and sell it. By this I cleared $1,000. the second year in Canada. We had noticed the year before that there was a great demand for hay, so why not supply this demand when thousands of acres of good haying land went to waste each year? This business I kept up first with Adolf Kuhn, but when the Kuhns left for the U.S.A. in 1930, I proceeded alone, hiring my help.

During my successful years in business I began to realize I needed an education. Until now I had never attended any school. During my childhood days in Russia there was always war; after I was able to work, I was busy making a living as per the story you have just read. Now I saw it was an absolute necessity for me to go to school, not that I at that time had any intention of going into the ministry. In fact, I had tried very hard to forget my vows made to my dying mother in the exile of Siberia, Russia – that if I grew up I would preach the Gospel. I had accepted the Lord in 1928, the second year I was in Canada. Of course, I had been a Christian when a child, but had lost out with God completely when working in the flour mill in Russia, and had signed up to be a Communist. I came back to the Lord as a penitent sinner when listening to a mighty gospel message preached in the little Baptist church at Lockwood. But there was one thing that hindered me in my Christian growth, and that was prosperity. $1,000 in the bank was not much indeed, but to me it was more than I ever had. Upon this I founded my future plans to become a business man in dry goods as soon as I got on my feet to start it.

The thing that hindered me most was lack of an education. In 1931 I invested most of my money in six good milk cows which I rented out to some farmer with the idea that each year each cow would bring me a calf and the farmer using my cow would raise that calf for me until it was one year old. In this manner I planned to get the ball rolling to put myself through school and college. This, my clever plan, failed me after my second year in school. The price of cattle went down so low that no farmer cared to even feed a cow, not only to milk her. I had to sell my cows at a tremendous loss. However, this did start me off to school and rather in a very nice way. As stated before, I never had grade one. I went to a high school known as the "German-English Academy" in Rosthern, Saskatchewan. I made my application for grade nine. The principal said to me, "How can you take grade nine when you have never taken grade one?" I persuaded him by saying it would look ridiculous for me, a 23 year old man, to start with grade one, so he took me on my own risk. He gave me a list of all the books I should get. I got a whole armful to them, but I did not know the difference between one book and the other. Books were books to me, and I could not read them. I would take my armful of books to my class periods and ask the students next to me, "What book is the teacher talking about?" They, of course, would find me the book and the page. Thus I kept on. Hard work! Let me tell you, if you never had even grade one and you are in a foreign country and then start in with grade nine, high school, you will find plenty to do. I tell you, I studied. Here is something that will surprise you. It did me. When the final exam came, I passed all my subjects except spelling, which I cannot do as yet.

 After the school term was over I went back to Lockwood. I was then driving my own car. I again started in my type of farming and running the business as described with my six milk cows. I managed to get enough together to go back for my grade ten. In the fall I was back in school, taking this time grade ten, plus two subjects in German and one subject in Greek on top of my full course of grade ten English. I assure you, I had another load. I studied practically day and night. No consideration was given to my tired body. I kept whipping myself to work.

After three months of slave-driving myself in this nature, my health gave way. I went to the doctor and he put me to bed in the hospital, telling me that I had 104 temperature and probably had that for days before I ever came to him. I had pneumonia. After recovery from this I went back to studying, this time trying to make up for lost time. In a short time my health gave way again. I then took the train to the nearest city where I could get an x-ray. I knew there was something dreadfully wrong with me. After the x-ray I was told I had T. B. (tuberculosis) and would have to go to the sanitarium for three years. This was a blow to me that just crushed me down so that I did not care to live. I used to walk on the street before I was moved to the sanitarium and cry out to the Lord, "Oh, my God, why hast thou forsaken me?" I blamed the Lord, telling Him that I had my share of suffering in my life during my childhood days, etc. All this did not seem to help in the least. I had to go to the sanitarium in Prince Alberta, Saskatchewan.

CHAPTER IV

In the Sanitarium

The word "peace" plays a very important part in our lives and it brings joy to our hearts when we hear it said. This is what I was listening for of the good Lord, for my heart indeed was in an upheaval when after the x-ray I was told I had T. B. I knew what that meant. There are many people in Russia with (Chachotka) tuberculosis and most of these people die very young, as there is no cure for it. In fact, I believe my mother had T. B., as she always was sickly and coughed a lot.

It was January 1933 when this discovery in my body was made. At once they signed me up for the sanitarium. I was only permitted to go back to school long enough to gather my things together. The Canadian government took over my expenses. I received a free ticket to Prince Albert, where there was a large sanitarium. Arriving there, I learned that even a taxi was provided for me to take me straight to the sanitarium from the railroad station.

Just a brief word of honor and respect to the Canadian government: I was greatly blessed when I saw this lovely one million dollar building with about 250 patients in it for treatment, and every one of them taken care of in the most helpful way they knew. However, to us who had been moved there as T. B. patients, it was a lonely place.

I was assigned a room and put to bed and told to stay in bed. At first I did not find it so hard, as I really was sick and, of course, the bed is the most comfortable place for sick folks. After a little rest, I began to feel quite well, and to my estimate I thought I could get up again. But this is not the case in the T. B. sanitarium.

When you once go to bed, you stay there for a long, long time. At my first x-ray I asked the doctor how long he thought I would have to stay in bed. "Oh," he said "about three years." I looked at him thinking that he was just fooling and took it rather with a grain of salt. When the next day my bed was pushed out on the balcony where about one hundred patients were strung out in a row, I learned, to my surprise, that the doctor actually meant what he said, for there were some there that had already been lying in bed for three and even more years trying to get rid of T. B. This was astounding to me. I had no idea that T. B. was such an enemy of humanity. In fact, I was told that T.B is incurable and that it is one of the oldest diseases known in human history whose germ was first discovered in 1882 by the famous German doctor Robert Koch, and was then named tuberculosis. Previous to that, it was known as "Phthisis" and incurable. What amazed me was that most of those patients in the sanitarium were young people like myself. No one really looked sick. They were all joking and happy and apparently enjoying their rest in bed just fine. The treatments were good, the food was excellent, and the nurses were very kind. Everything was done to make us feel happy and to forget our troubles. We were also told to keep busy doing something with our hands or reading and writing, etc. All this helped toward our recovery.

When I saw that I had lots of time I began to read. It was here where I first read the Bible through from cover to cover in the English language. Previous to that, I usually read the Bible in German. My eyes finally gave out on me and I was forbidden to read. Then I began to compose poetry and discovered the fact that I could compose. I composed many poems in the German language which appeared weekly in a German paper known as "Rundschau." Then I tried it in the English language and managed to get a few composed, too. Here is one of my poems composed for a little school girl.

ADVICE

If you are at school today,
Try to do just what they say.
Never sit and be distressed,
Be sincere and do your best.

If you are outside to play,
That's the time you should be gay.
Never stay behind the rest,
Be ahead and do your best.

If you are at home again,
Do your homework best you can.
Then go out for a pleasant walk,
And rest your mind till nine o'clock.

If you then go to your bed
With a clear and rested head,
Then the night be sweet to you,
And the morning cheerful, too.

If you keep what you now read,
I'm sure you will be glad.
Trust yourself and others too,
This is my advice to you.

Next I made a suitcase by lying straight on my back just working with my hands on top of the covers. This suitcase was made out of large x-ray film boxes and overlaid with leatherette and proved to be very strong. That suitcase served me later for five years in traveling with the Gospel.

After each three months the patients would receive an x-ray examination. When my turn came I told the doctor that I didn't expect to stay in the sanitarium for three years. I said to him "I know why I am here. I was supposed to preach the gospel as I promised my dying mother, but I tried to run away from God like Jonah of old and the Lord caused him to be swallowed up by the sea-monster. As soon as I consecrated my life to His service and quit this running around after earthly things, God will see to it that I will be out of here." The doctor looked at me and said "Are you superstitious?" I told him that I am far from being superstitious, but that I believed in a mighty God who is able to heal T. B. as well as any other thing. I went back to my room for the next three months. Of course, I was getting pneupthories, that is, my left lung was stopped from breathing. By air-pressure this was kept up every week for ten months. Twice every week I had to go to the operating room and have a large hollow needle go through my side right next to my lungs and then be pumped up with air to keep the lung in pressure.

When my next turn for x-ray came, the same doctor who asked me if I was superstitious said to me, "You have made a wonderful improvement these last three months." I told him that I had consecrated my life to the Lord and I am now willing to go and preach the Gospel and, of course, it is now up to the Lord to see to it that I get well. The doctor didn't say a word, he just smiled it off.

Another three months slipped by and I was again called for x-ray. By this time I had been flat on my back for one year. When the doctor looked at my x-ray he said that my lungs were completely closed in and all the cavities had healed. I told him that I believed it was the Lord that healed them in one year instead of three years as he thought. I was put on exercises to regain back my strength to walk, which by this time I had forgotten how to do. At my next turn of examination I was pronounced checked (cured) and I left the sanitarium in 16½ months instead of three years. All glory to His Wonderful Name!

During this time I felt the nearness of the precious Saviour so much that at times I thought I could just reach out and touch the Lord Jesus Christ who stood at my bedside. It was also here that I commenced to write this life story of mine, only I wrote it in German. In later years, at this present time of writing in 1948, I translated it into English.

Let me just say a word in honor to my wonderful Saviour, the Lord Jesus Christ. If it had not been for His nearness to me at that time, I would not be the same person in bodily appearance. The doctors thought that I should have an operation called "Thorocoplostic," which means they would take out chunks of ribs and collapse the one lung for good, thus of course, disfiguring the body. In my case I did not permit them to give me this operation, for I felt as if the Lord stood by me and promised to get me out of there without the operation. Glory to His precious Name!

During my stay in the sanitarium, I had visited the different departments of it, and just before I close with this chapter, I may say a few words of what I saw.

There is a ward where the bone T. B. patients are kept. This is rather a pathetic sight. There were many little children who had been lying in casts for many years in such a position that their little bodies could not move any direction. Also older folks were there for as many as 13 years, lying in the cast because of T. B. of the spine. I saw one man who had a very short body. His spine had shrunk seven and a half inches and the ribs tilted over his hips. Yet he was cured from T. B. and lived many, many years after.

Of course, there is a glow in these dark clouds of life, because behind the clouds there is sunshine. Through all my life I have found it to be so and particularly when the clouds are the darkest, the glow of the after sun is the brightest. I found that most of the T. B. patients are cheerful. This is none other than the Lord. I found people such as one young girl who was in the cast for three years after having part of her spine re-grafted. Yet, every time you saw her she had a smile on her face and was extremely busy with her hands. She was making doilies and selling them through some nurses. I was told that she could almost earn a living by this craft. As a rule you will find very busy people in the sanitarium, doing something with their hands. It is not the man that is a cripple that is to be pitied, but the one who will always pity himself and will not use the glorious opportunity coming his way. There was one dear brother in the Lord, "Jakob Unrau" who used to say, "Things that I cannot change I take along with patience and make the best of it." That is the kind of spirit we need to make this life worthwhile. This dear brother went home to be with the Lord after being in the sanitarium for 13 years. I am much indebted to Brother Unrau, who assisted me in the writing of this book.

There were some in contrast to this man, and no doubt some women, too, who just looked for an opportunity to disobey the rules of the sanitarium and as soon as the nurses were out of sight, they would carouse around in other rooms, play cards, and get sick the next day, etc. It was mostly this kind whom the undertaker took out of the sanitarium and not the taxi.

How I thank God for these wonderful experiences I had in the sanitarium. It gave me greater confidence in Christ my Lord Whom I serve. It also gave me a thankful heart to the government of Canada and the United States who are so helpful to their sick folks in making it possible for such treatments. In contrast to this type of government, we find it not so in the European rules of government, particularly in Soviet Russia where people are not helped when they are sick. The government demands of them whether sick or well to meet their obligations to the government. If they fail to pay their taxes and to render their amount of labor to the upkeep of the government, they are exiled to Siberia to die for punishment because they were not well enough to be of help to the government.

Let me just quote you a letter I received from my sister during the time I was in the sanitarium. This letter came from my half-sister who was living on our old farm, to which I had signed over the Hausmann estate in 1925 when visiting them as per chapter before explains. She writes:

"*Dear Marzelius,*

I have heard that you are still alive, so I will write to you and let you know of the condition we are in. Dear brother, if you have a heart and still love us, I beg of you, please help us. We have six children and are trying hard to keep them alive. Now they have put Albert (her husband) in jail to starve him for punishment because we were not able to pay our taxes. He has been in jail for three weeks and they are demanding of me to pay taxes or they will send him to Siberia to die, or to work the rest of his life for the government. Please help us. The children and I are starving at home and Albert in the hands of the government. Oh, help us please.   *Your Sister, Martha Roloff.*"

Upon receiving this letter I was almost helpless, being in the sanitarium a T. B. patient, but I wired them $10.00. I received word from them three months later and learned that Albert was sent to Siberia to work there till he died, and Martha with the children went through some-thing indescribable. The government came and took away everything they had, even every chicken and the only cow they had, so they faced starvation. By the time my money reached them, some of the children had already died; some were rescued or just prolonged their misery. I never heard of them since, but was told through others that anyone receiving help from America was counted a traitor to the Soviet government and was condemned to be shot.

From my brother I received a letter telling me that he was preaching the Gospel and was caught by the Soviet authorities and was threatened to be executed if ever he would preach again. He then fled to Central Asia among the Tartar race of people, Mohammedans in faith. I also sent him some help, but I haven't heard anything of him since 1935. His last address was from Central Asia among a race of people that resembled the Chinese and yet were white skinned people.

From my younger sister, Mathilda, who was then the wife of a Communist banker, I received a letter telling me that her husband was sick with tuberculosis. Though himself being a Communist, he didn't receive any help from the Soviet and he died shortly and left his young wife and two children helpless, facing a dire need in life. I sent her some help too, but I couldn't keep this up, as I myself was in bed with T. B. Oh, how I thank God that I was in America instead of in the "Red Paradise!"

During these years, 1933-1937, there was much being preached to the American people by some of these Dr. Jones and Browns who had gone to Moscow and came back to tell us what a wonderful government Russia had. According to the lectures we listened to of these men who had been as far as Moscow and had been blinded by Communism and carried around on their hands of deceit, it sounded as if Russia had already entered the millennium and Stalin was their Christ. Oh, how my heart burned within me against these devilish reports of so-called D. D.'s I cried to the Lord if He would let me out of the sanitarium, I would go from town to town and inform the people differently. This, my petition, was granted of the dear Lord, and I was dismissed from the sanitarium in May 1935 and was led of the good Lord through some schooling which equipped me for this ministry of the precious Gospel of our Lord Jesus Christ. All glory to His precious Name.

I am sure it would be of interest to you to know that in 1935, four hundred thousand were exiled to Siberia by Stalin because of the Name of Christ. Then in 1939, when the Second World War broke out, there were again exiled to Siberia four million people who were considered dangerous to the government. Altogether, according to the "Reader's Digest" in the April issue of 1947, there must have been at that time in the Soviet Slave Camps in Siberia fourteen million exiles. The type of labor they are doing there is well known to the writer personally, as I had seen these camps in 1916 when still under the Russian Czar's reign. The people, men and women alike, are sawing lumber in these Siberian oak forests to be shipped into foreign countries. In 1937, America, through private agencies, purchased several shiploads of this beautiful white oak lumber which was all sawed by the exiles in Siberia. It is the blood of the martyrs when you look upon your lovely white oak bleached furniture. Just remember it was prepared under the whip and the lash of the Communist by your brother and sister in Christ.

Oh, Russia, dark Russia. The blood is covering the entire surface thereof. It is truly the mystery of iniquity.

CHAPTER V

In the School of God

It was one day in May, 1935, that the head doctor of the sanitarium told me I was now ready to be dismissed from the sanitarium and that I could go home. Since the time I was admitted to the sanitarium to this particular day in May, I had spent 16½ months in the sanitarium.

It indeed was great joy to me to know that the T. B. was conquered and as you recall, this was not the first sickness I had conquered so far in my life. It sounded extremely good to me to go home – but I had no home to go to. My property, such as the milk cows I had, were all sold by this time and so were my four horses. You read in the chapter before that I sent money to my starving loved one in Russia. I obtained that money by selling through the mail and friends all my belongings I had stored up and placed in and around Lockwood, Saskatchewan. In fact, by this time, you could consider me financially broke. The only place I called home was the place I had worked last, at Mr. and Mrs. Hislop's place. I had worked for this farmer for five years and they did prove themselves to me very loving, in fact to the extent that I looked up to her as my mother. Moreover, all my extra clothing, etc., was at their place stored up somewhere. All this made it home to me.

When my release from the sanitarium was given me, I took the train homeward bound for the Hislop farm, not to start working again, but to receive the motherly care of Mrs. Hislop. Give honor to whom honor is due. Mr. and Mrs. Hislop truly did their share in making it a home for me. God bless them! For some time all I could do was to help in the house, wash dishes, etc. Mrs. Hislop taught me how to cook. She said to me, "Mark, I want to make a good husband out of you for some fine girl."

While being there, I had much time to pray. I used to go to a little bush where I could pray aloud asking the Lord to lead me to do something in order to earn some money so that I could again take up my training and this time with the intention of becoming a minister of the Gospel. Day after day I pursued the same thought of prayer in this little bush. Mr. and Mrs. Hislop knew about it, too.

One day coming home from my prayer time, I picked up the newspaper and looking through all the ads, which usually was my custom, to see if there was something to do for a man that could not work, I saw an ad which read in this wise: "A salesman wanted to sell tailor-made suits." I felt this ad was for me. I at once ordered the samples and started out selling suits. The Lord helping me, I sold suits everywhere, making sometimes as much as $15.00 a day. Mr. Hislop let me use his car to drive around in so I began to earn good money.

One day I was granted a wonderful opportunity of getting a free ride to Lansing, Michigan, to see my sister Olga. I found it hard to leave my newly established business, but Mr. Hislop thought I should take this opportunity, as it would greatly help me in my complete recovery. As I always took his advice as fatherly advice, I took this man from Detroit, Michigan up on his proposal to me and went along with him to Lansing. I had one of the fastest rides in a car I have ever had so far. He traveled 80 and 85 miles an hour.

Having obtained only three weeks' permit to be in the United States, I thought I would soon be back to my old job again. But while there, my brother-in-law extended my stay to three months, after which he and his family took a trip to Canada and I again had a very inexpensive ride back.

I thoroughly enjoyed my stay and visit with the Kuhns. They had a fine home. Adolf was then working in the General Motor's Oldsmobile factory and made good money.

After the three months expired I had to go back to Canada according to the law of immigration order. This brought me back to Lockwood right in the harvest season, the best time of the year to sell suits. I bought myself a Model T Ford and was on my route for business, making some three to five dollars profit in each sales transaction, and so clearing about $10.00 to $15.00 per day. This was wonderful. Shortly afterwards I bought myself a better car, a beautiful Model A roadster, 1928. I saw myself again getting up financially and according to my bank book I again had $800. in the back. Then one day I drove to Saskatoon for a T. B. check-up. To my astounding surprise the doctor told me that my T. B. was under control but that I had sugar diabetes and he advised me to change climate at once. He told me to go to the coast, (Vancouver) and eat lots of cherries and fresh fruit and leave sugar alone altogether. I went home and sold my lovely car, took the bus, and was on my way to Vancouver. Arriving in the fall, there was not much work for me to do. Work of my nature was not to be found there. So I started a business. I purchased a restaurant for $500. down payment and took a mortgage for the rest. This, however, was not the will of the Lord, for would I have succeeded in this business, I would again have forgotten my vows to preach the Gospel.

In about three months I was bankrupt. I signed my name on the dotted line and let the mortgage company take my business. By this time I felt myself going down in health rapidly. The trouble and worry was too much for me. My daily expense was heavy. I paid $35.00 for a room per month and boarded in restaurants. I looked for a job daily and found none. When I was right down and had sold my lovely Nash coupe for only $40.00, I threw myself on my face before God and asked Him for mercy and guidance. I went to Stanly Park and hid myself in that park amongst some trees so no one could ever find me, where I could pray aloud. Being on my knees before my Lord I received strength and new courage. Going back from the park I stopped in a large hotel and asked if they had any job for me. They said they had a job in the kitchen where they could employ a man right now. An hour later I was found in the kitchen, washing dishes with a washing machine. This I kept up until late spring, but the job was not good for my health; it was too steamy for T. B. lungs.

Having again saved $150 in the bank, I tried something else. I bought myself a 1927 Chevrolet and then went out and rented a cherry orchard of about 20 trees. I hired two boys to help me pick those cherries and I would load my Chevrolet down with all it could carry and go up to Vancouver and peddle these cherries from door to door. Let me assure you, there was good money in it. Moreover, I could follow my doctor's advice. I just simply lived on cherries and cured up my diabetes for good. In fact, I never took insulin and since 12 years ago I have never had any diabetes attacks. Apparently the juice of the cherries, with the help of the Lord, dissolved all the extra sugar in my body. Glory to His Wonderful Name. At that time I also started selling suits in the villages around Vancouver, but not as successfully as in Saskatchewan where there was no large city for hundreds of miles.

Having again brought my bank book up to $300 I looked for a job where I could make money faster. One day I got mixed up with a real estate man in the city. He advised me to become a shareholder in a logging concern. Not being very familiar with those so-called real estate men, I took him up on it and plunged in my $300 into this business. I was supposed to make $8.00 per day by hauling the logs to the water with a caterpillar which I knew how to operate and also my money I had invested would bring me 16% interest. Moreover, I would be amongst pine and cedar trees, which is the best place for a tubercular person to be.

I took the boat and went out to my new business on an island called "Sea Shell" north of Victory, British Columbia. Arriving there I located my camp. I found the workers at work. I thought I was one of the big shots. After a while I discovered that every one of those workers was just as much a big shot as I was. Everyone had the same investment in this business. For a few weeks I enjoyed it. The fresh air of the forest was lovely, but to my surprise, I discovered that this company was not really a company, but only a lovely dream of a shrewd real estate man and in the space of two months all of us workers and so-called shareholders were bankrupt and heading for home, if we had one.

I was tired of this up and down life. For a little season I made some money, and then I'd go broke again. I hid myself amongst those tall cedar trees and sank upon my knees before God. I confessed to Him that I had been chasing after the opportunities of life and trying to run away from His calling me to the ministry. Now here I was, just as Jonah was in the belly of the fish, and I cried to God for mercy to give me one more chance. At this time I had lost every bit of courage I had ever possessed. I begged and pleaded that God would not cast me aside, even as Jonah of old, and I made promises that I would perform my vows. "And the LORD spake unto the fish, and it vomited out Jonah upon the dry land." (Jonah 2:10). So was I again brought back to the city of Vancouver.

But what could I do? My capital consisted of $35.00 to my name. You cannot live very long on that amount in a city of that nature. In fact, I was afraid to rent a room, for there would have been nothing left of my $35.00 by the end of the week.

The Lord once again gave me new courage. Oh, I thank

God for the constant courage He poured upon me. I went to the car lots, bought me an old 1926 Chevrolet, went to the second-hand stores, and bought up a lot of junk such as old pants, suits, shoes, shirts, etc. for a dollar or two. You can fill your car with products of this nature, so I loaded my car down with junk, and then I filled her with gasoline and oil and was on my way to the country. After I was out of the city about 75 miles I visited the farmers and offered them a trade for potatoes, eggs, butter, and vegetables of all sorts. That day I converted all my materials to farmers' products and I make my way back to the city. Arriving there I went to the restaurants at the back door and sold my products to them with a good margin of gain. This I kept up every day for a month, and by that time, I was able to buy myself a decent car, a 1928 Model A, and I again could pull out my wallet fat with money.

This time I really meant business for the Lord. I wanted to go to a Bible school to take some training for the ministry. I felt led of the Lord to make my way back to Saskatchewan. I advertised for passengers so that my trip would not be a loss to me, but a gain. In but a matter of days I had four passengers to Saskatchewan and with my little Ford just overhauled, I faced the Rocky Mountains, bound for the prairies. Delivering my passengers to their respective places, I discovered that I was $35.00 to the good after paying for all my gas and oil. Next to that I had a very lovely trip out of the deal, climbing mountains to the extent that one of my lady passengers fainted for fear when at one place I turned a short corner at 25 miles an hour when we were 700 feet up.

Coming back to Lockwood, I started in at once selling suits and clearing my $10.00 to $15.00 a day. In but a little while I had some $300 to my name. At that same time the Lord opened a door for me to attend one of the best Bible Institutes in Canada. It was through a minister, Lee

Forsmark by name, whom I met and who also wrote the Foreword of this autobiography as you will notice on the front page, that this opportunity came. Rev. Forsmark, being a graduate of the Prairie Bible Institute, recommended it to me very highly. In fact, he wrote a recommendation letter for me to the principal of the school, Dr. Maxwell. This, however, he did because of the courtesy of his young wife who knew me from years before when yet a maiden and felt at liberty to introduce me to her husband as a good young man. I was very thankful to Rev. and Mrs. Lee Forsmark, who were then on their honeymoon, whom the Lord so wonderfully used to start me off in the right direction for His service.

CHAPTER VI

In the Prairie Bible Institute

It was in 1938 that I was on my way to the Prairie Bible Institute in Three Hills, Alberta, Canada. Arriving there I found a large school. There were 500 students enrolled. It was a very lovely set-up. The institute looked like a little city of its own. Moreover, it was on an independent basis. It had its own dairy, and its own bakery, its own farm to raise their vegetables, etc. All this was, and still is, operated by student power, each student contributing 1½ hours of labor out of every 24. Due to this fact the tuition, and room and board was very low. The total amount required for education, room and board, including laundry and a haircut wherever needed, was for the low price of $3.50 per week.

I started in on a three-year course, picking my subjects not really with the aim to graduate, but only to acquire some knowledge of how to preach the precious gospel of my dear Lord and Saviour Jesus Christ. I found my studies extremely hard, as I was troubled with sleeplessness and had already for one whole year been taking sleeping pills practically every night, almost turning out to be a drug addict. This, of course, beclouded my mind, but the only way I could fall asleep was by being doped to sleep.

In spite of this, I felt the Lord wanted me to organize a male gospel quartette which was to go out for the summer months to bring the gospel to the nation. I prayed much about this, asking the Lord for very definite guidance and asking Him to give me the right kind of men for the job. Now when the Lord does something, He always does it wonderfully. It so came to pass that these young men came to me in a very outstanding way without me urging or persuading them. All of them were very good singers. I was the only one who couldn't read notes. After each one of us had the assurance that the Lord was calling us to work, we organized what was known as the Prairie Bible Institute Gospel Quartette. It was composed of Joe Jesperen, Eric McMurry, Rob Summerville, and Mark Hausmann. Joe was our best musician. He would take me to a piano and pound some tunes into me, do, re, me, fa, etc. Day after day I had to go over the scale and hum and sing these notes. For three months we were at it whenever spare time permitted. I was to sing the second bass, so I just kept growling away on that everywhere. Joe was constantly after me to get it right. Finally, we had a nice set of quartette numbers all pat and practiced and we felt very much encouraged. Eric, our secretary, was appointed to work out a route for us and put a schedule through for four months with a meeting somewhere every day. This too was nicely accomplished through the courtesy of the registration office at P. B. I. who gave us the registration book. From that we found students living on our route through Alberta and British Columbia. Through these students we received the address of their churches and pastors and thus we made cont acts for 7,000 miles through Alberta and British Columbia, Canada, touching 67 different towns and cities. The complete schedule when made out called for 158 meetings to be held with every day set and appointed.

When we thought that everything was running very smoothly, trials come upon us. Joe Jespersen received a letter from home telling him that his father was very sick and was undergoing the seventh major operation, which meant that Joe was not able to go with the quartette, but must go home and take over his father's interest in business to support the family. We four boys were indeed very downcast, and we organized an all-night prayer meeting for Mr. Jespersen. This was done with the permission of the school faculty. A week later another letter came telling

Joe to go ahead with the quartette work, as his father was miraculously healed and the doctor refrained from performing that operation. In fact, he was then on his duty, feeling the strengthening of the Lord upon him.

Let me assure you this was joy to us four boys. However, somewhat later I took sick and was moved to the hospital for an appendicitis operation. This was done and ten days later I was back in my room at the school. No sooner had I recovered than I took the flu. The time for our gospel tour was also approaching. Satan was right there to tempt me sore, telling me that definitely it was God's will for me to quit the idea of the gospel quartette. In my fear and doubt I picked up my Bible and let it fall open. The verse I saw first was Isaiah 41:10. "Fear thou not; for I am with thee: be not dismayed; for I am thy God: I will strengthen thee; yea, I will help thee; yea, I will uphold thee with the right hand of my righteousness." Beloved reader, this was to me as if a funnel was set upon my head and blessings poured into me. I had my quartette boys come to my room and showing them this verse, I requested that they kneel down at my bedside and place their hands upon my and pray. This was faithfully done, and I got up, dressed, and went out to practice with the boys. All the fever was gone when I felt the touch of the Lord upon me.

We were praying for a little trailer to carry our suitcases. One day a man came to the service bringing a trailer with him and leaving it there. We looked at it and then agreed it was just what we needed. A few days later the man came back for it. Bob Summerville ran out and asked him if he would like to sell the trailer, as we would like to use it for the quartette work this summer. Instead of selling it to us he gave it to us. Just like the Lord! That is how God provides for His own.

Our time had come and we were fully equipped to go. We built a little roof over the trailer and printed on the roof in large letters "JESUS SAVES." In that way we traveled all that year, covering 7,000 miles, meeting 158 appointments, singing 400 quartette numbers, and over some 300 duets. Joe sang and played his piano-accordion over 300 solos. Each one of us took part in the preaching, and we had the triumphant joy of seeing 103 precious lost souls come to Christ. Glory! Glory to His Wonderful Name!

Besides this, a large number of young folks came to P. B. I. for training the following year. Some of them are now missionaries in the foreign field. Totaling the number of people we met and preached to that year were over 11,000 souls that heard us sing and preach the gospel. There were also some people we met that have meant very much in our lives as faithful prayer partners who are even now still praying for us. In my case, there was one young woman I met that year to whom I was introduced in the same manner as perhaps hundreds of them. At that particular time I thought no more of it, but this girl was one of those who came to P. B. I. the next year, and thus kept it up for three years and later became Mrs. Houseman. It indeed is wonderful how the Lord works in our lives, how we meet people, how the Lord brings things to pass in order to bless and comfort His children. Of this particular young lady, Isobel Hurlburt, you will read more in the chapters yet left for you to read.

Many wonderful incidents that have happened on this our gospel tour have just been mentioned because of the lack of space and time. Yet perhaps by far the most important things have not even been touched on. Let me tell you that many and precious were the experiences we four boys had during these four months of traveling for our Lord. Our experiences were of various types. Sometimes we went through hard trials, such as shortage of money, health or car trouble, for my old Model A was getting up in years. All these tests are not to be compared with the blessings that came after the trial was over. I recall one time my nerves threatened to give out on me. On top of it I received a bill from the doctor and the hospital for my operation which was in the amount of $155. At that time I thought I would give up, but there and then the Lord undertook. My health increased, the money came in, and the debt was paid. The triumph was great. I had three very faithful young men with me who stood with me in these trials, denying themselves any comfort or rest until we prayed through.

At one time we were completely out of money. We had three hundred miles to go and no gas in the car and no money in the purse. Right there and then a man walked up to us and asked us if we had been in a certain town, naming it to us. We said yes, for we had just recently held meetings in this town. He said, "My son is the preacher of that church," and he pulled out a $5.00 bill and gave it to us, not knowing of course that it was the Lord who compelled him to do this. At another place we were in need of $40.00 to make a certain payment. We prayed about it and then coming home to our room where we stayed, we found an envelope with $40.00 in it. We knew not who it was that put it there; neither had anyone heard that we were in need of this amount.

One of the greatest blessings we had was when we labored at the Burrard Inlet Bible Camp. Many precious young lives came to Jesus. What a joy it is to lead souls to Christ! Should someone ask us if we lacked anything, with the disciples of old we would have to admit, we lacked nothing. Starting out on a 7,000 mile tour without a dollar between us and coming to the end rejoicing and triumphant, having all our expenses paid and money to spare, is indeed of the Lord.

When the tour was ended each went to his respective home and appointment. I, personally, went back as far as the Okanogan Valley, British Columbia, where I helped in the apple harvest to earn money for my next term at school. I also preached at many places on my way back, receiving offerings to help pay my next year's board at P.B.I. I traveled alone on the journey from Vancouver, British Columbia, where we ended our tour, pulling a half-ton of apples in my little trailer across the mountains from the Okanogan Valley to Three Hills, Alberta. All Glory to His Name!

CHAPTER VII

Back to P. B. I.

Coming back to P. B. I. in 1940 and feeling much refreshed and strengthened from the blessed experiences of the summer, I rejoicingly took my next year's courses. My health at this time was much better. I certainly count it a great privilege to have been able to attend Prairie Bible Institute, to be under teachers such as we had there. It makes a person feel like the Apostle Paul who thought it a great privilege to sit at the feet of Gamaliel, one of the greatest teachers in his day. I shall never forget the powerful messages given by Mr. Maxwell, the principal of the Institute. All the other teaching which was given to us by this God-chosen staff of teachers was presented to us in such a way that in every lesson and in every class period the finger of God was moving and stirring our hearts. The Bible literally lived before us. Oh, what a book this wonderful Bible of ours really is!

During these months the Lord again pressed it upon my heart to go out with a quartette. Again I started praying for three young men chosen of the Lord for this job, and these indeed were given. One day mentioning it to a young man by the name of Norman Jamisen, I immediately felt that he was one of God's choices for my quartette. So now there were two of us praying for this work. The Bible teaches, "...That if two of you shall agree on earth as touching any thing that they shall ask, it shall be done to them of my Father which is in heaven." (Matthew 18:19). So Norman and I prayed. The Lord sent in first Charles Harnstra, second tenor; then Clare McElheren, first tenor; Norman baritone; and I bass. You see, the Lord had taken my first quartette of boys to mission fields. Joe Jespersen was in Cuba, Eric McMurry in China, and Bob Summerville was at that time in the northern territories of Canada, but at the present time of writing, he is on his way to India.

After the school term was over, our new group launched out, having worked a route through Alberta and Saskatchewan as far north as the Canadian roads would permit us to go. I can assure you, dear reader, that we boys had a blessed time. I am not saying that all things ran without a trial, but the blessed part of Christian life is to overcome trials and to triumph over difficulties. Many were the difficulties that faced us boys. One great trouble on our hands was that old Ford of mine. It took us where we wanted to go, but complained, and as you know, each complaint of a car costs money.

The next outstanding trial we had to face was the muddy roads in Saskatchewan. For miles we boys would be plowing through mud and pushing the car and taking off the wheels and scraping out the potter's clay so that they would turn again. Thus it went on practically all that summer. Yet beloved, these trials are not to be compared with the joy that was ours of leading precious souls to the foot of the cross. Sixty-seven I find recorded in my book that took a stand for Jesus. All glory to His Name!

Again these boys were dispersed to their God-appointed fields of labor. Clare McElheren became pastor of a Nazarene church in my home town in Lockwood, Saskatchewan. Charles Harnstra at present is the pastor of a church in DeBolt in the Peace River block, Alberta. Norman Jamisen and I came back for another year of training at P. B. I.

On our way home we stopped at a town to take in the wheat harvest in order to earn some money for our next term at school. Having acquired the needed amount, we again were on our way to Three Hills, Alberta. Arriving there we saw a great improvement. The buildings had been enlarged and added more to the already city-like Bible Institute. The registration of students had by this time increased to 700. As Mr. Maxwell says, "The growing pains of P. B. I. are great."

As you usually find it the first week at school after registration for a new term, it is rather confusing and running to and fro. By the time the second week was well in the harness we were glued to our desks. This was to be my last year, not that I at the end of the term would qualify for graduation, but it would complete my course to become a minister of the Gospel, having taken all the required points in doctrine and Bible study.

This year of 1940 and 1941 at P. B. I. was a hard year. There was very much sickness throughout the school. Sometimes an entire floor of a dormitory was converted into a hospital ward. The measles epidemic was laying low all those who did not have them when they were small. Other sicknesses of different types also caused many disturbances that winter.

Once again I felt the Lord wanted me to pursue in the Gospel quartette work. The Lord brought me to my knees to pray for three young men to go with me. This time my heart stretched out toward the East, if possible as far as Winnipeg, Manitoba. One by one these young men were chosen by the Lord. Truly it was of His wonderful choice, for I could never have chosen such splendid men as made up this quartette. The first tenor was Jacob Dyck, a man who had outstanding qualities to sing; the second tenor, David Hart, an excellent singer and preacher. The baritone, Victor Long, was a qualified singer, preacher and also a good mechanic for my old Ford. (All three of these young men are out in the foreign fields as missionaries now. Jacob is in India, David in Haiti, and Victor in South America, doing exploits for the Lord. God bless them!)

The practicing of new songs came much easier now, seeing that I had the practice from the years before. Joe

Jespersen, from the first quartette, had the hardest time with me, as in that year I didn't know anything about notes. The only thing I knew about them was that they were black and the paper was white. If there ever was a wrong fellow starting up a quartette, it was I. I practically was tone deaf, but I knew it was of the Lord. According to the scriptures, God does choose the foolish things and uses them. That gave me great courage to go through with it. It always was that way in my life. I would start something absolutely out of my line, contrary to my nature, and God would bless it, which is just like Him. He knows how to handle and use foolish things.

That winter we gave my old Ford an overhauling and also the trailer. When next April came around and it was time for us to leave, we were all set. The only thing was that we had no license for the car as yet, and it was about time to leave. I had no money to my name, not even to buy a free lunch. We prayed that the Lord would please send us the $12.00 needed for a car license and a driver's license. This was kept up until almost the day we were to leave, but still we had no money and no licenses. One day Brother Victor came to my room rather broke down, and said, "I guess the Lord will not send in any money as long as there is money amongst us boys," and I said, "Indeed not." He said, "Well, I am greatly convicted about it; I have $15.00 on me." I said, "Well, that is fine. Then the Lord did answer our prayers in convicting you about it. Let's go and get the car and driver's licenses." We were all equipped, car license, trailer license, and four drivers' licenses, all out of that $15.00 with one dollar left for gasoline to start off with. Glory! We were on our way for another four or five months of blessed work with the Lord.

We covered half of Alberta and went clear through Saskatchewan and down to Winnipeg, covering 8,000 miles that summer. We started April 10th at Three Hills,

Alberta, and ended August 21st at Winnipeg, Manitoba. What a time! We sang over 500 quartettes, Jac and Dave sang over 200 duets, also Jac and Victor sang around some 100 duets, and Vic and Dave must have sang at least 150 solos apiece. All of us preached that year in equal terms. We had joy of leading 225 precious souls to Christ, young and old alike, but most of them teenagers. It was one of the most successful summers of my life.

All three boys remained with me on the way back as far as Jacob Dyck's place at Main Center, Saskatchewan. Here we dispersed. Dave went back to Spokane, Washington and from there to the foreign field of Haiti. Victor went to his home in Alberta, and I went back to start an Evangelistic Campaign in Enchant, Alberta.

By the time we dispersed we had traveled over 9,000 miles, had covered every cent of the expenses, and each one of us had received about $100 throughout the five months with blessings untold. To God be the Glory!

No wonder the Apostle Paul could say to the church at Philippi when they thought they were in need, "But my God shall supply all your needs according to his riches in glory by Christ Jesus." (Philippians 4:19). To the honor of my Saviour's dear Name, after these three years of experience, I want to join in the words of the dear old Apostle Paul who said to the church at Ephesus, "Now unto him that is able to do exceeding abundantly above all that we ask or think, according to the power that worketh in us, unto him be glory in the church by Christ Jesus through all ages, world without end. Amen." (Ephesians 3:20-21).

CHAPTER VIII

The Year of My Ordination

In 1941 requests came in to Mr. Maxwell's office to recommend some young man that would qualify for ordination as minister of the Gospel. My name was included amongst the twelve who were recommended to the Evangelical Free Church of Canada. The leading man in this request for prospective young ministers was Rev. Lee Forsmark, then of Enchant, Alberta. This is the same Rev. Forsmark who had also started me off in the Prairie Bible Institute. By this time I had made good acquaintance with this brother and he had requested that at the return of my quartette tour I should come to Enchant for an evangelistic campaign. On my return in the month of August this proposal began to materialize. Rev. Forsmark started me off at different towns together with a dear brother who was up for the same test, namely Alex McComb. Many and precious were the meetings we two held, particularly at a little town, Sholdise, and a larger town, Arrowwood. Here at Arrowwood I took over to serve a church known as the "Church of Christ."

Feeling my needs in this my new undertaking, I sent in a special request of prayer to the Prairie Bible Institute. This was presented to the students as an urgent request and faithfully followed up by all those who believe in the power of prayer. Particularly I learned later of one young lady whose name appeared before, Isobel Hurlburt, who prayed for me every day that whole winter through. At school I did not pay any more particular attention to Isobel than to all the rest of the ladies. First, of course, because it is against the rules of the school to chum with females, and next because I did not know her any more than many others, with the exception that I knew she was a fine young woman who loved the Lord and was planning to be a missionary in Africa. However, I noticed many times Isobel smiling very attractively at me, which is the only means of communication at P. B. I., that of smiles and eye language. Of this, no doubt, many young folks were guilty of; for ever so many marriages came from P. B. I., this so-called extremely strict Bible school.

My labor at Arrowwood later on resulted that I was asked of the Free Church if I would care to be ordained. Indeed I did care for this, for by this time I saw my calling, and my heart was set to be a minister of the Gospel for the rest of my life.

On November 12, 1941, which also is my birthday, I had the great privilege with nine other young men from P.B. I. to present ourselves before the board of ordination which was set up by Rev. Lee Forsmark, to take place in the little town of Ensign, where different churches had gathered to witness this great act to transpire. It was no small occasion to set ten young men aside for the ministry of the Gospel. To me, and no doubt to the rest of my fellow-students, it was a day that shall never be forgotten. For this particular occasion I had purchased for myself a beautiful large "Scofield Bible" to have it ordained together with me in the ministry. It was requested of us young men to kneel in a circle, after all the preliminaries and questions were finished, and place our Bibles under our knees. Thus we ten young men knelt on our Bibles before the Lord in the assemble, and by the laying on of hands of the other ministers, we were dedicated and ordained into the glorious fight for precious lost souls for which my Saviour died.

After my ordination I labored around in Southern Alberta for all that winter and part of the spring. I had blessed experiences during that time seeing precious souls come to the Lord. There is one thing outstanding in my life that I want you to know. During my ministry I was attacked by an uncomfortable feeling that undermined my balance of standing on my feet, even to such an extent that I would have to HOLD TIGHT TO THE PULPIT when I preached lest I would fall down. But my mind was clear. I went to the clinic in Lathridge, Alberta, and had a real check-up of different doctors. No particular sickness was found by them. Then I was sent to the ear specialist and as soon as he looked into my ears he began to whistle and said to me, "Young man, all I think of your life is as a man who has a revolver set to his head and a bad man at the other end of it. It might pop any time."

You see ever since five years of age, when I had scarlet fever, I had a running ear and that had gone on by this time for 28 years. Sometimes pus would just be oozing out of my ear. Now the ear specialist told me that all the hearing organs were gone (of course, I always was deaf in that ear) and that my balancing box was attacked and that I most probably would get a stroke or just drop over and die, as there was only the thickness of a sheet of paper left of the bone between the brain and the air.

I testified to this doctor, telling him that I indeed was very happy, I was a Christian, and if my life would pop, I would pop right into the arms of Jesus. He was interested in this cool-nerved testimony and listened to me preach to him for half an hour. He also received a Gospel of John and some tracts from my hands with the promise to me that he would read them.

After having received my prescription and the needed medicine, I went back to my place where I held meetings in a country place. That night at my service I told the people what the doctor had told me. Right there and then there was much prayer going up to the throne of grace for my ear. At the place where I stayed there was a very devout couple who loved the Lord with all their hearts. This couple

(I learned later was an elderly couple) were up all night praying for me. I did not know it and I went to bed. In the morning I woke up and my ear was dry for the first time in many years. No sign of pus or bad odor was detected.

A few weeks later I went back to this doctor. He looked into my ear, turned and looked at me for a while and said, "A remarkable change has taken place in your ear." I told him about the prayers that were offered up for it. He, of course not being a saved man, could not see with me eye to eye, telling me it was the powder he gave me. I said to him that I had only used it once, as I really had no more use for it, seeing that my ear was perfectly dry. Thus I left his office with the doctor perplexed and wondering, but not admitting that it was God who had healed it. To Him be the glory. Now it is seven years since, and my ear has been perfectly well. In fact, much hearing has come back to me; so much so that I can take a telephone message and hear it perfectly well. Do you, my dear reader, know this great physician for body and soul? I recommend Him to you. He is wonderful!

Shortly after this experience I received a call to come to the Peace River Bible Institute in Sexsmith, Peace River, Alberta. This was approximately 1,000 miles away from where I was then. Feeling it to be of the Lord, I checked up my old Ford and was on my way. It was in those days in Canada when tire rationing was on, as well as gasoline rationing. Coming to the city of Edmonton, I had to get a new tire, or I could never set out on my next 500 miles. Try as I may by all different governmental rights, I was unable to buy either tire or tube. Bringing it to the Lord in prayer, I met a man who directed me to an office in the parliament building where consideration is given to ministers of the Gospel. Here I was given a license, and by presenting it to a dealer who had tires and tubes in stock, they could sell me one of each. This was soon accomplished, for the dealers who had stock were not permitted to sell unless such documents were presented.

The last trip to the Peace River was heavy going amid severe mud practically all the way. At one place my car showed me that my gas was very low. The large zero, as it does on a Model A, stood before me, and my map showed yet 40 miles to the next town. There was at that time a Christian young woman in my car who had caught a ride with me. I explained to her our condition that we would soon be stranded and out of gas, and on those roads there was very little traffic those days. So we both prayed about it and I kept on going as far as we could go. Thus I kept on and on. According to all proofs and facts of the car, there was not a drop of gas in the tank. I said to Esther, "You must keep your eyes on Jesus; never mind that zero." Thus we drove for those 40 miles. Arriving in that little town, I saw a gas station and turning my car to it, the engine stopped while the car coasted to the tank. All Glory to His wonderful Name! He that watches over the sparrow watches over me.

Arriving at the Peace River Bible Institute, I was appointed a job to join a team in tent work. This team was composed of two of the teachers of the school, Mrs. Stephenson, an elderly lady; Rev. Don Masterton; Ruth Dyer, who is now a missionary in India; and myself; making four of us. We used to go into a place, pitch a tent, and while Rev. Don Masterson and I did this work, the ladies would canvass the country around about, visiting every home and invite people for the meetings at night. Many and precious were the experiences we had. There were trials to face. There were triumphs to enjoy.

At one place we met up with a caterpillar epidemic. Every tree was stripped of its leaves. The ground was covered to such an extent that you would think you walked on a carpet. Next to this we had the mosquitoes so thick that you could not sit down except there was a strong smudge. Sleeping, of course, was only possible under nets, and then you woke up in the morning finding squashed caterpillars on your pillow, etc. The women slept in the trailer house and Don and I in a little tent. What a time we had fighting mosquitoes and picking off caterpillars that crawled on us! But there were blessed experiences of leading precious souls to Christ. An entire book could be written on those experiences, but I shall only touch on the very main points, lest you get weary reading it.

One incident that happened I shall never forget. We were moving to our next appointment. These appointments were made by Rev. Walter McNoughton, the dean of the Bible Institute. This next appointment was leading us through very hilly country. We were on our journey for a half day when we came into the mountain regions near Fort St. John and Dawson Creek on the highway that leads to Alaska. We attempted to climb one of these mountains with our little Model A (one of the school cars) and a large house-trailer behind loaded with many things, and next to that there were five of us in the car, four women and myself. When halfway up the hill my car gave up, I tried the brakes to hold her but it overpowered me. I saw the whole outfit going backwards down the hill. I let out a holler, "We are lost; jump!" This was for once that women folks obeyed me better than ever before in my life. Out piled those women fast as lightning. Seeing them all standing on the road safe and sound, I turned the wheel just in time before the plunge to clear the road for me, and I jumped. Down rolled our outfit, 35 feet, trailer and car. I stood at the brink watching them roll down. When everything had settled, I ran down and stopped the engine, for the car was not badly damaged. You see when the trailer hitch broke off, it gave the car such a kick that she flew ahead and hit the rock wall with the bumper and then came backwards over the cliff, not touching the ground. When it landed, the trailer had already settled, and therefore cushioned the landing of the car.

The first thing I did was to get one of the five bicycles out of the wreckage and pedal back to the town we just had left behind and report it to the police. I also hired a truck to take the wreckage to the next town where some Christian friends lived whom our party knew. As for the car, all that was wrong was one wheel broken where it had landed, and the door from which I had jumped flew off. As for the trailer, it was all in splinters. Inside of it, clothing, suits, etc. were all mixed with jam and butter and whatnot, piled into the same stew. The truck took all the belongings but left the remains of the trailer. I got the car back on the road and drove it behind him. There we folks settled down for two weeks. Rev. Masterson was on his way by train because of the overloaded car. Catching up with us, he had no small surprise.

However, we two at once set out to build a new trailer house. In two weeks we were finished and ready to go on our way. Again we launched forth, this time only the four previously mentioned going. I had Don Masterson take his car back and bring my own to hook it up to the new trailer. Again we were facing high mountains and whenever we came to one, the two ladies, Mrs. Stephenson and Miss Dyer, refused to remain in the car, but rather preferred walking as Mr. Masterson and I drove it up. At one place I said to Ruth, "Here, take this block, and when you see the car stalling on me, put the block under the wheel." When I was halfway up I looked back and saw poor Ruth running for all she was worth, trying to keep up with the car in case it stopped. She jumped out too soon.

At another place I gave the block to Don, who sat beside me ready to jump in case the car stopped, to put the block under it. He got his hand caught under the block and what a condition that was. We managed to release his hand and the ladies dressed it. No bones were broken. Thanks be to God!

Then we hired a farmer with a tractor to pull our trailer up the hill. We finally came to a river where we had to take the ferry. After crossing the river we could not make the steep rise from the ferry to the shore. The ferry man got angry and said, "get this junk out of here." But I could not, having too big a load, so a jeep hooked on to my car and he could not pull it. Then a large International truck hooked on to the front of the jeep, telling me to get hold of my wheel. He just jerked my outfit out of there with a crash, breaking my poor old car asunder at the rear frame. Oh, what a trial! The car was broken again. I got myself some wire and wired the frame that held the hitch together and thus we pulled the trailer house another 60 miles and finally reached our destination. Arriving there we were told that there was an epidemic of chickenpox and we could not hold meetings. We went back to the next town and pitched our tents. In the process of a week six souls had come to Christ. This took the sting out of all the rough experiences we had. All glory be to His Name! One soul is worth more than worlds.

Altogether during that campaign in the Peace River we had good results. I had the privilege of seeing precious souls come to Christ, particularly during the winter time when I had evangelistic campaigns all around the Peace River. At one place I had the joy of seeing 21 march forward to the altar, weeping their way to Jesus. I kept this type of work up all that summer and winter until March 1943, when a great change took place in my life.

During all the time in the Peace River, I was corresponding with Isobel Hurlburt. Having made some acquaintance with her when on my way to the Peace River, I stopped at P. B. I. for the Conference which was then going on. I ran across Isobel again and she met me with her sweet smiles which were not so easy to forget. When at work in the Peace River, I sent out circular letters to all my prayer partners and of course, to her too, upon which I received a very lovely letter which led to correspondence between us. Let me assure you, my dear reader, you cannot do this for too long a time with young ladies until they have cornered you so that you feel compelled to pop the question. This happened and the result of it you may guess.

By this time I thought I was quite safe from ever getting hooked. I was then 34 years old and no girl ever had the nerve to ask me and neither did I have the nerve to ask her. You know a man is never safe as long as there are girls in this world. Who ever knew that a 22 year old lassie would spin such a lonely net with her letters and smiles that old (Saint) Mark would get tangled up – but that is just what happened.

After our decisions had been made and the date for the wedding set, we made up a lovely wedding announcement letter, and after my bride-to-be had agreed to its contents, it was sent back to me to be printed, of which 500 copies were enveloped and scattered around through Canada, blazing the unheard news that a lovely young girl was casting in her lot with this shouting, noisy preacher, Mark Houseman.

I sold my car and took the train to Kamloops, British Columbia, (about 1500 miles) to meet my bride-to-be. Glory!

CHAPTER IX

No More I, But "We"

March 5th, 1943 I left the Peace River from the little station, High Prairie, bound for Kamloops, British Columbia. When at Edmonton I stopped off to purchase several things needed for this occasion.

A very outstanding thing happened before I took this trip. When laboring in that country I was very low financially, and my places of meetings were not of the nature where you may expect much money to come into the preacher's hands. When it seemed clear to me that Isobel and I should get married, I made a bargain with the Lord.

I prayed for a very definite sign if this marriage was of Him. To prove it to me I asked the Lord to send me $100 by a certain date, over and above all my expenses as to the rings and wedding suits, etc., including also all my travel expense to Kamloops. In other words, when I got there I should have $100 left over, not counting the price I got for my car, for that I would need again to buy another car. This $100 I asked of the Lord to let us have our honeymoon. I said to the Lord that if that money would not come in at that set date, I would postpone our marriage until more definite guidance was given of Him. It may sound peculiar to you, but at that set date, I had $160 to my name and two lovely brand new suits so that my bride-to-be could choose which one she wanted me to wear for that great event. The engagement ring as well as the wedding ring was paid for. In fact, I had new clothing from shoes to hat and underwear. All the way through I was one hundred percent dressed. When I had paid for my ticket I still had $25.00 over the hundred I had asked for. This I knew was given me to buy presents for Isobel and her grandma, with whom she stayed at that time. Isobel at that time was nursing in a T. B. sanitarium in Tranquille, British Columbia and lived with her grandmother at Kamloops. She had been raised by her grandmother from her young childhood and had been given to her by her mother for that purpose.

I arrived at Kamloops three day before the great day. Twelve o' clock that night, three days before our marriage, at the railroad station I, for the first time in our lives, gathered Isobel into my arms. What a thrill! A taxi took us to grandma's home and for the first time I met old Grandma Hurlburt. In that little four-room house I found presents displayed from one end to the other which were sent there by all of our friends due to these 500 wedding letters sent out. Next a large box of mail was presented to me. Over some 300 letters were to be opened. However, we did not start in on them that night, for my lap and arms were loaded down with my lovely bride-to-be.

During our correspondence, when assured in our hearts that we soon would be on our honeymoon, I made out a large Gospel tour starting at Vancouver, British Columbia. One week after the wedding we would go through all the provinces of British Columbia, Alberta and Saskatchewan for six months, converting our honeymoon into a Gospel-moon.

The next day we two started on that stack of letters. What a day! It took all that day and then some, but our hearts were exceedingly glad and uplifted when we realized that out of these letters we gathered somewhat over $200 in cash and untold greetings wishing God's richest blessings upon us. All the lovely presents before our eyes made our hearts leap for joy. It is wonderful, beloved, to have so many Christian friends. At that time I carried a four hundred correspondence list and Isobel about a hundred. Combining the two, we had a rich correspondence.

Finally March 10th, seven o'clock had arrived. All that day I was forbidden to see my sweet girl. In reward for this day of agony she was placed into my arms as the sweetest gift next to my salvation that was ever given to me, even as my darling wife. The reception was held in a lovely large home with friends since grandma's house was too small for such a purpose.

After being driven around in a beautiful car with tin cans tied to it, we settled down for the night with grandma. In fact, for the first two days, we stayed with grandma. Then we set out for our Gospel-moon.

During these two days we did not do as other young folks do and forget about all the duties for a while; instead we answered letters every hour of the day. Next to this, Mrs. Houseman and I went uptown to pay bills. The hundred dollars I asked of the Lord when in Peace River was to be used for this purpose, for Isobel's folks were not in a position to pay for our wedding and neither was Isobel or I, but the Lord was, and He proved Himself faithful in every detail.

The third day after our wedding we were on our way to Vancouver, British Columbia. Arriving there we started to look for a car, for before us was a 10,000 mile trip and a six months' schedule to sing and preach the gospel through the western province of Canada. It was no small undertaking in those days of war even to think of buying a car. Tires were rationed very closely and gas was rationed to such an extent that even local ministers had to do a lot of walking so that their gas would hold out.

After a long search for a car we located a car that was for sale with four new tires on it with the body all caved in, having been hit by a truck. The price of it was $375. With the price I got for my old Ford and other money, we were able to pay $200 down and the rest in monthly payments. We bought this car and had it straightened out. When it came out of the body-shop it looked like a brand new one, except that it was a 1934 Chevrolet instead of a 1943. Now, how could we obtain the gas? I went to the authorities and they told me that evangelistic work was non-essential and no gas would be granted to us. We went home and spread these matters before the Lord. Then we wrote a letter, also signed by one of the leading pastors in Vancouver, and sent this to Victoria, British Columbia. While it was on its way we did much praying that God would over-rule human laws and send us forth to preach the gospel. After three days we witnessed the manifestation of God's great faithfulness when a gas-ration book arrived to us, category C, which really was a doctor's category. This was exceedingly abundant above all that we had asked. We had sufficient gasoline and some to spare. All glory be to His wonderful Name!

Our services began. All the month of March and half through April we had appointments in and around Vancouver. What a time! The Lord had now established our goings. Every night and Sundays we held two or three meetings somewhere. Isobel sang one or two solos at each service, and perhaps we would sing one or two duets. I would call on Isobel to speak to the children for a little while, after which I would preach. Oh, the joy of seeing precious souls come to Christ on this, our so-called honeymoon! The good Lord provided for our needs.

Many were our blessings and enjoyments on this, our Gospel-moon. We travelled over the highest mountains in the Canadian Rockies, seeing some of the most wonderful things in nature. A complete book could be written about this trip. I believe it was one of the longest and blessed honeymoons any young couple ever had. However, during that time sorrow and testing also came upon us. It apparently was too much for Isobel, not being used to travel as much as I was. Then, of course, every day or every other day a new place and a new bed was indeed very hard on nerves.

However, it was a trip neither of us shall ever forget. We had what you may call good times such as climbing mountains, seeing sights, etc.; but above all, what I call the good times was when we had the joy of leading precious lost souls to Jesus. This was our great privilege many dozen times over. All glory be to His wonderful Name!

We also had the privilege of attending several church conferences during which our appointments for the future were made. The Evangelical Free Church appointed us a place for service somewhere in center Saskatchewan in a little town called Fosston. We were to take over this field right after our gospel tour. This gospel tour finally ended September 3rd in the city of Edmonton, Alberta. We were bound for Fosston to our new appointment, new endeavor, and new responsibilities.

CHAPTER X

Pastor's Family

We were very glad indeed when we finally finished our tour. Many very faithful friends were made on this tour. Even at this present time, five years hence, we are convinced there are some of these dear friends that we had made acquaintance with that are still praying for us.

Arriving at Fosston about 9 p. m. we soon located the church. The town was small with about 200 people, two large Catholic churches, and this little church of ours built on the outskirts of the town with a little parsonage alongside of it. It was locked, but looking through the windows we could see our home for years to come. We then located the church deacon, Mr. Denham, who was also the principal of the Fosston High School. Having introduced ourselves to him, we soon felt at home. The next day we took possession of our new home.

It was not too bad for a home at that. We found four fairly large rooms in this parsonage – two bedrooms, a dining room and a kitchen. It was a struggle to begin with and indeed a new experience to us to get furniture, but the people, being very kind, helped us exceedingly. I soon took to building and added a storm porch to the back of the parsonage. I also built a garage for our well-used Chevy. The next summer I built a large woodshed. The church also agreed to finish the church building, which until now was not completed inside. I appealed for help to our conference and obtained $1,000 to finish my two churches. The other church we served was eight miles south of us in a little town called Hendon. Much carpenter work and painting plus the church work was at hand.

During that time the Lord had laid upon my heart to start a Bible Camp. For a long time we looked for a suitable place. Finding a place near Wadena at a little lake known as the Fishing Lake, we and the Baptist Church of Wadena ventured into this new endeavor and bought 11½ acres of shore, a lovely place. You could not but see the hand of God in it. We bought the finest place on the lake for $45.00 which was half of the original price asked. People were astounded and would have paid us twice or perhaps four times the price for it. Yes, my dear reader, that is just how God does things. He is a God of miracles.

We got a dear Christian brother, Norman Austring, a truck owner, interested in it. In a little while we had all the building materials there, so we started our building. Everything was built out of rustic slabs except the frames. Rev. Fugelson, pastor of the Baptist church and I, plus some very fine helpers, set that camp up in but two months, having constructed one building to be used as a Tabernacle and dining hall, 15 by 50 feet; two dormitories 12 by 24 feet; a kitchen 12 by 24 feet; and a cellar and an 18 foot well. We were all set for the enrollment at camp time, July 15th, with one hundred and twenty youngsters enrolled. Over fifty took a stand for Christ. All glory to His wonderful Name! While at Fosston we had Grandma Hurlburt come to us, hoping that would be her permanent home as she was then 77 years old. It was also at Fosston, Saskatchewan, where little Margaret Isobel, our first child, was born May 18, 1944. Grandma proved to be a wonderful help to us with the little one.

After the birth of the child my wife was very sick, having many different troubles and complications which indeed marred our family happiness that we had enjoyed when we were strong and healthy. One and a half years later on September 14, 1945, little Walter Mark was born, with the hope, according to the doctor's advice, that now Mrs. Houseman's trouble would mend. This, however, was not the case, but it turned for the worse. We do, in spite of it all, thank God for the little ones we now have. What a blessing they can be in the midst of their mischievousness and tricks they will play.

For two and a half years we labored at Fosston, having had a very fine group of people to work with. The people were predominantly Norwegian, active and hard-working people, willing to sacrifice and to share what they had with others.

In October, 1946, we were asked if we would like to take up a field in northern Minnesota in the U. S. A. This appealed to us, and talking matters over with grandma, who was tired of the cold Saskatchewan winters and wanted to go back to British Columbia, we found there was nothing that tied us down, so we gave our consent.

While being at Fosston I found it too large a field for me to handle alone and by the agreement of my church there was sent to us an assistant pastor, my dear old friend, Rev. Alex McComb, with whom I worked before. This dear brother, being yet single, was cornered by a very fine young lady, one of the school teachers in the town. As usual when that happens a young man loses his power to say "no" and so instead of it a very emphatic "yes" was said by both of them, and they were married. This shortly proved most definitely of the Lord. As we made our application for the immigration to the States, brother and sister McComb became the pastor family of Fosston and Hendon. All glory to His wonderful Name!

CHAPTER XI

In the United States of America

Having resigned from our church, we then set out to obtain our needed documents for immigration. This was not as easy as one may think, and for almost six months we were at it until at last we had our visa to cross the border.

During this time of waiting we stayed with a fine family on a farm, Mr. and Mrs. I. Austring who had a family of 12 children, of which the greater number were still home. What a lively time we had in that house when our two were added to the gang. Every week-end my wife and I went to Wadena, leaving our youngsters in the hands of Grandma Austring. There in the Baptist church in Wadena there was no pastor at that time, as Rev. Fugelson had resigned, so I just filled the pulpit for those six months of our waiting. In fact, we could have accepted the call to that church had not our hearts been set for the United States.

On April 15th, 1946 we finally had all our needed documents. Mr. Austring loaded all our belongings on a farmer's grain wagon and thus for seven miles we drove through the mud as you may suspect it to be in Saskatchewan. We indeed owe much appreciation and thanks to this fine family who were to us like parents.

Loading on the train at Hendon, our first stop for further investigation in regards to our permission to cross the border was Winnipeg. For two days we were questioned back and forth at the Winnipeg immigration office until we finally received our supreme authority to cross the line.

Our destiny in the United States was Holt, Minnesota. We were to take over two churches there, one in Holt and the other in Strathcona. The place that had been secured for renting as our temporary living quarters was gone when we arrived because of our extreme long delay of coming. A very lovely family in the county of Holt, Mr. and Mrs. T. B. Foldon, took us to their home where we again were treated as if we were their own children. During our four months of stay there the Strathcona church commenced building a parsonage for us. We therefore moved into the back of the church in order to be handy to help in this construction work. The Lord's people were kind and worked hard to get this parsonage up.

Things, however, had risen which were disagreeable, upon which I thought it wise to give my resignation, being convinced in my heart that somebody else could do a better work for the Lord in this particular place than I could.

During that time we received a call to serve at the Roseau Baptist Church, having our release from Strathcona. This we gladly accepted and moved to Roseau, Minnesota, on March 2, 1947. We were very thankful to the good Lord for this fine place of labor and lovely dwelling place that we enjoy. We have the finest home we have had in our married life and indeed a very fine group of people to work with, predominately a Swedish community.

Moreover it was here at Roseau where we were once more blessed with a little one, Josephine Agnes, born March 29, 1949. Shortly after the birth of Josephine, Mrs. Houseman had to undergo her second major operation. Truly we have much reason to praise God, even in those testing days. We realized then, more than ever, why the Lord brought us to Roseau. Here we had one of the greatest surgeons (Dr. Berge) that you could ever hope to find in the world. And not only was he good as to his profession, but also he was sympathetic to those that were in the ministry of the Lord, not charging anything for his fine labor. Give honor to whom honor is due! We had both of our older children's tonsils removed, Josephine was born there, and my wife had her successful operation there which meant one and a half hours on the operating table and not a cent was charged. I rejoice that at the present time my wife is what you call a healthy and happy mother of three lovely children. Moreover, let me speak for myself; I could never find words sufficient to express my thanks to the guiding hand of our dear Lord during my life both when in childhood and as a single young man and also now as a father of three children and husband of a fine Christ-loving wife.

Now, my dear reader, my story has come to an end right to the present time of writing. Personally, I am glad I am finished, for I have many other things to do, such as each pastor will find. Next to this, my pastoral work, I am engaged in building a trailer house which will be used when traveling around with the precious Gospel story.

Just for a brief moment looking back upon my life, can you visualize what you have just read in the chapters before? Can you see that little ragged boy without a home, without father or mother, roaming around the streets of a large city in the exile of Siberia, Russia, half-starved, literally wrapped in rags, and covered with dirt and lice, and now standing before the public in a respectable manner preaching the unsearchable riches of Christ? How is all this made possible? All because of a loving Saviour and a Godly praying mother. Glory be to His most wonderful Name! If you, my dear reader, do not know Jesus, this wonderful Saviour and friend, won't you just right now, after having read this life story of mine, slip down on your knees and ask Him to be your Saviour and thus permit Him to answer the prayer of your Christian mother?

"Wherefore he is able also to save them to the uttermost that come unto God by him, seeing he ever liveth to make intercession for them." (Hebrew 7:25).

"Come now, and let us reason together, saith the Lord, though your sins be as scarlet they shall be as white as snow; though they be red like crimson, they shall be as wool." (Isaiah 1:8).

Should you be a Christian and feel distressed and perplexed in your life, after reading my story which is full of trials and perplexities, I recommend you to Him who in such hours spoke to me with Isaiah 41: 10, "Fear thou not; for I am with thee: be not dismayed; for I am thy God: I will strengthen thee; yea, I will help thee; yea, I will uphold thee with the right hand of my righteousness."

My last words in the writing of this book, and I trust the last minute of my life, are and shall be "Glory to His wonderful, Precious Name!"

CHAPTER XII

The Last Chapter

This last chapter was written seven years later. All these years since 1948 I was trying to get this story on the market for you people to read. But because of the shortage of money and, of course, because I had no rich uncle, I just could not get it before the public. However, in this year of 1954 I felt led of the Lord to send a circular to all my friends that had given me their name and address to send to them a book as soon as it is off the press. I sent out three thousand letters. At the present date I have sufficient returns with advance pay for their book to give orders to the press to start printing.

Will you please permit me now to take you back to the days of Roseau, Minnesota, since it was here where the good Lord greatly blessed us? It was here where our last little sweetheart, Josephine Agnes, was born. At this time of my writing she is now five years old. If you would like to see her, just turn to the last family picture; and there she is, and very mischievous, too. Never, no never, shall we forget Roseau, Minnesota. Until this present day we always compare all our places with Roseau, for it was the finest place in our ministry so far. Then too, it was here where it placed the Lord to take us through much testing. Mrs. Houseman had a very severe operation here, but she came through victorious. We had a very capable surgeon, Dr. Berge, to perform the operation. With the help of God Mrs. Houseman has been quite well ever since.

Now, just to give you a brief account between 1950 and 1955, I must say we did very much traveling. For a while we were the pastor family in the First Baptist Church at International Falls, Minnesota. Then it was our intention to go out as missionaries to South America, and for this reason we moved to California. Between the time that we resigned from our pastorate and the missionary career, we lived for eight months in Minneapolis, Minnesota. I took a little training in hospital work, and for this reason I became an orderly at the University Hospital of Minneapolis. Every day I worked with the sick folk and dead bodies in the morgue. I helped in the post-mortem. For Sundays we were always booked to preach somewhere, so my wife and kiddies came along to help daddy preach the gospel in song. During this time we scheduled a Gospel tour for us across the United States, from Minnesota to Michigan, and then down to Kentucky, Missouri, Kansas, Colorado, and finally to Chico, California, where we became students at Boots Camp under the New Tribes Mission. However, in the month of September, I felt definitely compelled of the Lord to go to Washington, D. C. to assist the Russian Bible Society to get Russian Bibles to Europe. From September of 1952 to July 1953 I really put the miles behind me. In these ten months I added 35,000 miles on the speedometer. I preached in 224 different churches all through the states of Maryland, Pennsylvania, and New York.

At the same time I was looking every day in many different towns to rent a home for my family. The Lord so led that I found a place and we settled down in Shamokin, Pennsylvania. I got the tickets for them to board the train at Sacramento, California to come to Shamokin, Pennsylvania, clear across the United States. After being separated two months from them it was a real blessing to be together again. Shamokin, Pennsylvania, by the way, is a large town of 35,000 population. It is a mining town and rough in every respect. I may say this, "where sin abounds, grace much more abounds," for this town has more good gospel preaching than any other town of its size I ever came across.

And now, my dear reader, seeing that you have endured reading this book so far, you may just as well keep on to the end, for here comes a very interesting account.

On the 8th of July 1953, I jumped on a plane for Europe. Eight thousand Russian Bibles were shipped to Europe by the Russian Bible Society. Pastor Malof, who is President of the Society, Rev. T. K. Youzva, and I were commissioned to go across to deliver these into the hands of Russian speaking people that had fled from behind the Iron Curtain.

Our plane ride was wonderful and exciting, but short. Seventeen hours after we were lifted from the New York airport we landed at Hamburg, Germany. Indeed this was a modern way of traveling. While we were away up in the sky hanging over the Atlantic Ocean I asked the plane authorities if I could have permission to preach the Gospel to the 70 passengers on board. This was granted, and I stepped before the people with my open Bible in hand. May I say here that this was the most thrilling experience I ever had in all my ministry. Here we were, away up in the sky over the ocean, moving along at 350 miles per hour, and let me tell you I could really open up with the truth, for no one dared to run out on me, even though perhaps some would have felt like it.

We had three stop-off places: Newfoundland, Ireland, and Scotland before our destiny of Hamburg, Germany. For the first week we were all three together, but after this Pastor Malof and Rev. Youzva left for France, Sweden, and Finland. My job was to finish the work in Germany; then go to Italy, Yugoslavia, and Switzerland.

May I say in a very few words (for at this point I could write a whole book, double the size of the one you are now reading) if you have never yet thanked God that you are living in America, you owe God an apology. There just is no country in all the world that has such liberty and so bountiful of everything for human life as North America. I was in many different countries in my life, and I say these words of personal conviction and experience.

God's Word says, "In the last days there will be a famine, not for bread or water, but for my word saith the Lord." This I personally saw being fulfilled in Europe. Our Bibles were very graciously received. My worst regret was that our Bibles were only in the Russian language. Many times I wished I would have had Bibles in every language in the world, for hands of every nation were stretched out for them. I also wish that we would have had 80,000 instead of only 8,000.

Until now I had but very little trouble to get along in Europe, for I speak different languages and could converse with all that I met. But when I came to Italy, none of my seven languages did me any good. Those Italians expected me to understand and speak in Italian. Italian is a foreign language to me. The only way I could express myself to them was with my hands and feet.

"Rome," yes, my friends. For all the things I saw in Rome, you will have to wait for my next book, "Visions of Europe." There I shall dwell on my experience beyond the sea. From Rome I flew to Trieste, Yugoslavia. Here too, as in all the other places in Europe, I found thousands of refugees who had miraculously escaped from behind the Iron Curtain. Yes, beloved Americans, people of every race, nation, and age will flee from the Soviet Union's "Paradise," so called, as a soul likes to flee from death. If you ever thought Communism had something to offer to the world, let me tell you what it is. It is death, destruction, misery, fear, and a perfect example of Hell.

In Trieste I stayed less than a week, contacting different refugee camps. My Bibles were all gone by now, so I just took names and addresses of people that wanted one. Later we sent them a Bible by mail from Washington, D.C.

Again I chartered a plane and this time for Switzerland. Give honor to whom honor is due, and this is just what I must say about Switzerland. Switzerland is the most beautiful and cleanest country I have ever seen. If you are a young man and are thinking of taking your bride for a nice honeymoon, just take her to Switzerland, the land of beauty and charm. Unfortunately for me, by the time I got to Switzerland I was so low on money (over and above my return ticket) that I could only stay for two days. I chartered the Swiss Atlantic Airplane leaving there in the mid-afternoon and what do you think? Well, at 9 o'clock the next morning our plane bulldozed its way out of the clouds above and settled right down at the New York Airport in the United States of America. Truly this is the greatest and most free country in the world to live. Needless for me to say, I found the shortest bus connection for home. Praise be to God. I arrived home into the arms of my loved ones all safe and sound, but a much more sobered-down man in my heart, realizing the needs of humanity.

Home sweet home, such as it was, in the mining town. After all, it is not the place or house you live in that makes the home, but the ones you love around you.

Again I pursued my evangelistic travels under the auspices of the Russian Bible Society. By the help of God, I put 32,000 miles on the speedometer of our then brand new little Henry J, preaching in 239 different churches spread over an area from Pennsylvania to Florida. Most of the time I was alone, but sometimes I had the family with me. Many friends were made and lost souls were reached during the time that this last chapter engulfs. All praise and glory belongs to our loving Saviour, the Lord Jesus Christ, who called me out of darkness into His marvelous light. It was He who held my hand from the days of my birth, as this book revealed it to you. He has never failed and never will. At present we are looking forward to once again settling down as a pastor family somewhere in a church of His choice. We hear Him say, "Sit down and rest a little while." I believe it will be our privilege to shepherd a flock somewhere soon. Calls have already come in from different churches in need of a pastor. With great longing in my heart, I look forward to being together with my family.

It shall always be said by these lips of clay, "For to me to live is Christ, and to die is gain." (Philippians 1:21).

The End

Epilogue

Our father, Mark Houseman, died on July 30th, 1958. He was 49 years old. But God used him for His purposes and His glory. We children shall always remember him as a loving father. Margaret was 14, Walter 13, and Josie was 9 years old when the Lord called Daddy home. It now has been 60 years and still his godly life is continuing to impact readers.

Josie wrote a sequel of his life called "Answered Prayer." It starts with Daddy still alive and tells about his death and how it impacted the family. Mother and each one of us children were greatly affected. But yet, Daddy's testimony of his love for God lives on in each one of our hearts.

Josephine   Walter   Margaret

THE HOUSEMAN FAMILY
Mark Isobel
Margaret Josephine Walter

THE HOUSEMAN FAMILY   Isobel   Josephine   Walter   Margaret   Mark
WE THANK GOD FOR PRAYER PARTNERS

"Brethern, my heart's desire and prayer to God for Israel, (Russia) is that they might be saved." But How shall they be saved, without the Bible? Yes, therefore the Lord hath laid it upon my heart, to be one of those that shall take the precious Word of God to them.

As you will pray, we-Pastor Basil Malof, President of the Russian Bible Society and Rev. T. K. Youzva, vice president and myself, the field secretary, are starting for Europe; this early part of the year 1953 with 10,000 of the complete Russian Bibles to be distributed among the Russian people behind the Iron Curtain, as well as among the many thousands of refugees from the Soviets, scattered in the refugee camps in Germany and other countries.

My family as you see on the picture shall remain here in U. S. A. But they too are in need of your daily prayers for it will be hard for the wife to be both mother and dad to the children while I am gone. Christ alone can feel the vacancy.

As for information to you of our present abode, the family address now is
1038 WEST MULBERRY STREET   SHAMOKIN, PA.
while the headquarters of *RUSSIAN BIBLE SOCIETY* remains
P. O. BOX 2709, WASHINGTON, D. C.

Yours in the Glorious fight for precious lost souls.   Mark.

Rev. Mark Houseman and His Family, taken in 1954. Phil. 1:21.

The Houseman Family

Walter, Josephine, Margaret, Mother and Dad. Yes, you are looking at the one's for whom you have been praying for years. All through our lives we were upheld and sustained, in much traveling, preaching, in testings and trials, all because of our faithful prayer partners. Thank God for prayer partners. Now since we became the field representatives of the **Hanbury Homes for Orphans** in Jamaica, we ever so much more depend on you, faithful co-laborers in the service of our Lord. To you who are new members to the Houseman prayer family, I would like to make known this our new step of faith. Not so long ago, I was positive I heard the Lord calling me to a different type of work. Up until August, 1957, we were nicely located as a pastor family in a lovely little church in the scenic state of New Hampshire. The Lord there spoke to me clear and plain, "Mark, move on". I said "Where to, Lord?" "Abraham went out, not knowing whither he went", was the answer. So I said, "Lord, here am I, send me." In just a few days I was over in Jamaica, B.W.I. It was here that I said to those missionaries, "Yes, I will be your field representative in the United States for the **Hanbury Homes for Orphans**". By the end of that month we moved to Berne, Indiana, into a rented home, trusting the Lord for every step we shall take. Now as your prayer object and Evangelist to many churches, I stand before you at the request of our Lord, saying to you, "Brethren, PRAY FOR US!"

As ever yours in the glorious fight for precious lost souls,

Mark Houseman

―Our Most Important Number Published

IMPORTANT BIBLE DISTRIBUTION REPORT FROM EUROPE

BIBLES FOR RUSSIA

OFFICIAL ORGAN OF THE RUSSIAN BIBLE SOCIETY, INC.

Mail address for all Correspondence and gifts: Russian Bible Society, Inc., P. O. Box 2709, Washington, D. C.

Published quarterly at 1400 New Hampshire Ave., N. W., Washington, D. C. Entered as second class matter at the Post Office at Washington 13, D. C., under the Act of March 3, 1879, and authorized January 11, 1950.

The Russian Bible Society was originally established in St. Petersburg, Russia, in 1813, by the Russian Emperor Alexander the First, the Conqueror of Napoleon, with Prince Golitzin as its first President. It was closed down in 1826 through the instigation of reactionary court elements by the Czar Nikolas the First, and remained abolished for 118 years. The Society was reorganized under the religious liberty of the Stars and Stripes of the United States of America, and incorporated in Washington, D. C., December 1944, as an American non-profit religious organization for the world-wide evangelization of the Russian people everywhere. The exiled Russian Church leader, Pastor Basil A. Malof, who had been tried in the Kremlin of Moscow for his Gospel work, and sentenced to Siberia, became the President of the reorganized Society. The Society has as its immediate objective the printing of one million Russian Bibles, five million New Testaments and Psalms, and twenty-five million copies of Gospel portions. Two hundred million Russian people are waiting for the word of God.

Vol. 4, No. 3   JULY-SEPT., 1953   25c per year. 5c per copy

The Russian Bible Society presents a full Russian Bible to the Archbishop Filofei in the Russian Cathedral of Hamburg, Germany, July, 1953, and to the officiating priest Ambrosius. These two Bibles were donated by two American Christian Friends. Standing, left to right: Baron Wrangel, Field Secretary Houseman, the Archbishop's Secretary Hartman, and the Archbishop, priest Ambrosius, Pastor Malof, Field Secretary T. K. Youzva.

Rev. Mark Houseman

Evangelist Mark Houseman

After You Have Read this book, and would like to have the author speak in your church either on his experiences or in an Evangelistic Campaign, you may feel free to write to him; but because of evangelistic travels and uncertain address, it would be wise that you address your letter in care of The Prairie Bible Institute, Three Hills, Alberta, Canada, or Economy Printing Concern, Inc., Berne, Indiana, through which you will always be able to get in touch with him, regardless if he is in America or Europe.

Evangelist Mark Houseman
After You Have Read this book, and would like to have the author speak in your church either on his experiences or in an Evangelistic Campaign, you may feel free to write to him; but because of evangelistic travels and uncertain address, it would be wise that you address your letter in care of The Prairie Bible Institute, Three Hills, Alberta, Canada, or c-o Russian Bible Society, P.O. Box 2709, Washington, D.C., through which you will always be able to get in touch with him, regardless if he is in America or Europe.

Made in the USA
Columbia, SC
04 February 2018